21st-CENTURY PSYCHOS

21st-Century Psychos

The Most Horrifying Killers of the Modern Era

Al Cimino

Al Cimino is a journalist and author who specializes in history and crime. His books include *Serial Killers*, *Drug Wars*, *Monsters Who Murder*, *Women Who Kill*, *Ted Bundy* and *The Story of the SS* among others.

This edition published in 2026 by Arcturus Publishing Limited
26/27 Bickels Yard, 151–153 Bermondsey Street,
London SE1 3HA

AD011239UK
Supplier 44, Date 0126

Printed in the US

CONTENTS

Introduction

It could be argued that the 1970s was the golden age of serial killers. Young people moved out from home and took to the road, often hitchhiking, which made them vulnerable. Not only that, but the US Supreme Court struck down the death penalty in 1972 as unconstitutional, though it has gradually been re-introduced. It meant that a lot of convicted murderers remained alive in prison, where they could be studied by psychologists and FBI profilers.

While old-fashioned serial killing – where the killer stalks his prey and picks them off one by one – has not gone away, it is easier now for a psycho to buy an assault rifle and blast away in a school, a shopping mall or a church, murder dozens, then turn the gun on themselves or die in a shoot-out with the police. And that's what lots of killers do in the 21st century. Any account of why they do it must be second hand, though some write long justifications or shoot videos, which they send to TV stations or post on the internet – another 21st-century phenomenon.

Mass murder is, of course, principally a male trait, except in the case of certain nurses. While they may be similarly deranged, that seems to me to be the subject for another book.

The question remains: what are we to make of these individuals who transgress against the most fundamental law of human civilization? All cultures and all religions have strictures against killing. Admittedly, some states sanction it in certain circumstances – in war or for the perpetrators of the most heinous crimes. But they forbid the individual from taking the power of the state into their own hands except in the most extreme cases – self-defence, where one could reasonably be in fear of one's own life or if the lives of others are in peril.

However, out there in the big, bad world, as we shall see, there are psychos who actually enjoy the act of killing and do it for sheer pleasure. Others harbour perverse sexual motivations. They rape, then kill the victim to remove the principal witness. Or, perhaps, they are necrophiliac and want to have sex with the dead body of those they have killed. And it gets far worse than that, I'm warning you.

Then, there are those who seek vengeance – perhaps against the whole world or even life itself. Mass murder becomes an existential statement. They are saying: 'I don't value my life, so I don't value yours either.'

They might direct this against a peer group, a particular type of people, or may fancy that they are taking a revolutionary stand against consumerism by murdering people innocently going about their shopping.

In a banal and empty life, maybe you might want to make one huge statement before you die. Serial killers often relish following their murderous careers in the media. They even measure themselves against others who have trodden that path.

For the disenchanted youth, slaughtering your schoolmates might be seen as the only way you are going to make the news headlines. The plodding, pedestrian choice of developing a talent or working hard to make something of yourself is just too much bother. Instead, grab an AK-47 and wipe out ten, 20, 50… and instant fame is yours.

The problem is that, whatever the motive, these people are human beings like you and me. Isn't there a little bit in all of us that wants to rebel against the world and blow it all away? You have to ask yourself under what circumstances would you take off down that road. Would you have to be seriously unstitched? Or would the urge come to you in dreams? What would happen if you found yourself plagued by psychopathic fantasies?

Murder, rape and other transgressions are the stuff of fantasy. Books, films and plays are full of such things. Agatha Christie made a lucrative career out of it. As we speak, novelists and scriptwriters are torturing their brains for some new angle on the unspeakable. Unfortunately, psycho killers are out there doing the same thing – only for real.

Now for the usual warnings that must accompany this sort of book. There are scenes of violence and passages of a sexual nature. Psychos are not usually very PC. Rapists tend to be sexists. Murders sometimes have racist or anti-semitic motives. There again, spree killers are inclusive and embrace diversity. They will kill anyone.

And there is a special warning for pedants – and on this point I am one – the 21st century started on 1 January 2001 as there was no year 0. But as all the big millennial celebrations started at midnight on 31 December 1999 (I blame Prince), I will start this book in 2000.

Al Cimino

CHAPTER 1

Abbas al-Baqir Abbas

8 December 2000

It was a Friday night during Ramadan at about 9pm when 33-year-old lone gunman, Abbas al-Baqir Abbas, burst into the al-Sunna al-Mohammediyya Mosque in Jaraffa, on the outskirts of Omdurman in Sudan, with an AK-47 assault rifle. He began shooting at the people in 'deep prayer', instantly killing at least 20 worshippers and wounding many more.

'There was blood all over the place; people were terrified,' said one worshipper.

According to witnesses, he deliberately avoided targeting the women's section of the mosque and told a fleeing woman that he was only shooting men. When he refused to surrender, there was a brief shoot-out with the police and Abbas was killed. More than 33 victims were wounded in the attack, among them a police officer. Ambulances and private cars were used to rush the wounded to hospital. Some were in a critical condition and at least two of the injured later died of their wounds.

Deadly rain

Witness Ahmed Mohammed Ali had tears in his eyes as he told Sudanese television that bullets rained down from three sides before a five-minute lull, following which he heard even heavier gunfire.

The police insisted that Abbas had acted alone, dismissing reports that shots were fired from three directions and that there had been at least three attackers dressed in jellabiyas, all but one fleeing before police arrived. There were also reports that not only had worshippers at the mosque been attacked, but that the gunman had rampaged through the nearby village, killing at least two boys.

Later, higher casualty figure were reported, some as high as 27 people killed and 53 wounded. An angry crowd demanding revenge gathered outside Omdurman University Hospital, where the casualties were taken.

The entire male population of the village turned out the following day to dig a mass grave, since Islamic tradition requires the dead be buried within a day. Bodies were carried to the graveyard wrapped in blankets on a bedstead. Newspapers reported that 18 bodies had been identified and that the authorities were due to carry out funerals.

Religious fanatic

Abbas al-Baqir Abbas was from Al-Dasis in the northern part of Sudan's Al Jazirah region. His uncle disclosed that his mother had left their home due to his religious fanaticism and that he beat his sister, accusing her of infidelity. He studied Economics at Tripoli University but was forced to leave Libya when the authorities began to fear that the Islamist group he led was a threat to security. Later, he served in the Popular Defence Forces, undergoing military training to fight the anti-government rebels waging a 17-year civil war in the southern part of Sudan.

Abbas had once been a member of insurgent group, Ansar al-Sunna, but had left over religious differences and joined the Muslim extremist group Takfir wal-Hijra, which means 'Atonement and Self-Denial' or 'Repentance and Flight', though its fuller meaning is 'repent your sins and flee the sinful world'. The name was used in Egypt in the early 1970s by a violent offshoot of the Muslim Brotherhood. Since then, the name has periodically been revived by groups in other Arab countries. It is known to have been active recently in Algeria and Jordan. A group using the name was thought to have plotted to assassinate Osama bin Laden in 1996 for being insufficiently radical. It is thought that there was a link between Takfir wal-Hijra and the group that bombed commuter trains in Madrid in 2004.

Originating in Egypt, Takfir wal-Hijra believes that the Sharia, or Islamic law, that rules in Sudan should be imposed by force, while the pacifist Ansar al-Sunna – 'Supporters of the Rules of the Prophet' – do not, despite being linked to the hardline Wahhabi sect, the dominant religious force in Saudi Arabia. This dispute had led to earlier shootings.

Takfir wal-Hijra advocates armed battle against Jews, Christians and apostate Muslims to restore the unity of the Islamic world order under a Caliph, who rules according to Sharia. The group's warriors are allowed to disguise their true principles to blend in with Western society and destroy it from within. These warriors will be martyrs in paradise after death.

On 4 February 1994, three assailants – Mohammed Abdullah al-Khilaifi, a Libyan Islamist, along with two Sudanese – attacked another Ansar al-Sunna mosque in Al Thawra with assault rifles, killing 19 people and injuring 15. Al-Khilaifi was later sentenced to death and executed on 19 September 1994. On 1 January 1996, eight assailants and a police officer were killed in a fight between members of the group and police in Kambo Ashara, when they tried to force villagers to convert. An armed assault on the same mosque in Jaraffa that Abbas would attack four years later left 12 people dead. On 1 November 1997, two members of Takfir wal-Hijra attacked people leaving a mosque in Arkawit with knives, killing two and wounding a further ten.

The independent *Al-Rai Al-Aam* newspaper reported that Abbas had previously threatened the congregation with an attack similar to the one in Al Thawra in 1994. The mosque's prayer leader, Beshir Ibrahim, told the *Akhbar Al-Yom* newspaper that the assailant was well-known in the village and had broken away from the Ansar al-Sunna.

This led to his arrest in 1998. He was detained for four months. He was arrested again a few months before the shooting, along with 20 other people suspected of being members of Takfir wal-Hijra. However, when they recanted and claimed they had left the group, they were released.

Power politics

The attack on Jaraffa took place just three days before general elections in Sudan, which were being boycotted by numerous opposition groups. However, observers said the dispute between Takfir wal-Hijra and Ansar al-Sunna was purely religious and that there was no connection between the attack and the vote for president and parliament.

The day after the shooting, the President of Sudan, Omar al-Bashir, visited the mosque to offer his condolences to relatives of the victims and assure them that legislation would be passed to control fanatical religious groups. He vowed 'to rectify laws in order to protect society from destructive and harmful ideas'.

In the wake of the massacre, police and security forces were deployed in Khartoum State in a major campaign to prevent further violence. With the election won, 65 leading members of Takfir wal-Hijra were arrested and the security laws were tightened, allowing suspects to be detained for up to six months. Opposition parties accused President al-Bashir of using the incident to curtail civil liberties and increase his power.

On 4 March 2009, an arrest warrant was issued for President al-Bashir by the International Criminal Court on two counts of war crimes and five counts of crimes against humanity. However, it was ruled that there was insufficient evidence to prosecute him for genocide over the campaign of murder, rape and deportation in Darfur.

In April 2019, he was ousted from the presidency by a military coup. The ruling Sudanese military council agreed to hand him over to the ICC after he was tried for corruption and money-laundering.

CHAPTER 2

Asanda Baninzi

June–August 2001

On 3 August 2004, 21-year-old Asanda Baninzi pleaded guilty to 14 murders, three attempted murders, 15 kidnappings, 12 robberies with aggravating circumstances, one indecent assault, four rapes, one housebreaking and the illegal possession of firearms and ammunition in South Africa. His co-accused, Mthuthezeli Eric Nombewu, also known as 'Wox', committed suicide after soldiers, police and angry residents surrounded his Gugulethu township shack in a six-hour siege.

Aged 18 when they began their killing spree, Baninzi and Wox smoked the hypnotic sedative Mandrax 'daily and as often as we could'.

'Neither Wox nor I worked and we needed money to live and to buy Mandrax and other drugs,' he said. 'To get money, we decided to hijack cars, so that we could kidnap the occupants and rob them of their money and personal effects, and so that we could strip the cars and sell the parts.'

Baninzi claimed that Wox and three other men who were being tried separately actually pulled the trigger, but he knew what they were going to do.

'I actively participated in the hijacking, kidnapping, robberies and rapes as I wanted to buy Mandrax tablets and I acknowledge that I unlawfully and intentionally committed murders and other crimes,' he said.

Baninzi said he knew what he had done had been unlawful and wrong. Although he had smoked Mandrax, he had been aware at all times of what he was doing. Most victims were shot execution-style in the back of the head.

'I am very ashamed of what I have done and deeply regret the pain and suffering that my actions have caused to the families and friends of the victims,' he said.

Life of crime

The first six charges against Baninzi related to an incident on 20 June 2001 when he and Wox hijacked a couple in their VW Microbus at their home in Gugulethu. One of the two men indecently assaulted the woman, before both of them raped her twice and robbed her and her male friend.

A further three charges related to the murders of taxi driver, Mogamat Brand, and his passenger, Ryan Masetu. Soon afterwards, the body of Mqibalo Mninsi was found lying beside the road. He had been shot in the head.

Baninzi admitted that, on 22 July, he and Wox hijacked Richard Dantjies and Faith Qwelane at gunpoint.

'We drove to the Zwelitsha area where we both raped the woman. I locked the man in the boot of the car,' he said. 'When we finished raping the woman, we took the couple to an unused shack in Nyanga. Wox shot them both in the head. We took their money, a cell phone and their VW.'

Baninzi admitted he had hijacked Stanley Khumalo and Ntombhekya Matomana, who were parked in Gugulethu on 25 July. The couple were kidnapped, shot and left for dead.

Baninzi said he and Nombewu had driven Ayanda Bokweni and Linda Mbabisa to the Mawumawu area in Nyanga after hijacking them on 8 August. Nombewu then shot Bokweni as he lay face down on the road, with a terrified Mbabisa still in the car. She was then taken to Zwelitsha, where she was raped by both Baninzi and Nombewu. Afterwards, she was fatally shot in the head.

Eager to buy Mandrax with the proceeds, Baninzi and Nombewu drove to a Gugulethu shebeen. Nombewu decided they would rob Mtiki, the alleged dealer.

'When we arrived, we pretended to be the police and shouted that she should open the door. When a woman opened the door, we pretended that we wanted to buy Mandrax tablets. When she said that she did not have any, we pointed our guns at her and robbed her of her money. Wox then shot her in the head, killing her,' said Baninzi.

Difficult path

Hoping for mitigation during Baninzi's sentencing, his advocate, Keith Hutton, begged the court to recommend that his client's sentence be coupled with counselling. 'He is, in many ways, just a lonely and frightened young man who got stuck on a path that was very difficult to get off.'

He was given 19 life sentences, plus a further 189 years.

'I have handled many cases in my career, but this is one where one person was charged with so many crimes – and admitted to committing them,' said investigating officer, Detective Inspector Jonathan Morris.

Baninzi was also convicted of murdering a ten-year-old girl, her teenage sister and their parents, bringing the tally to 18. Only a few days before they were murdered in August 2001, the Adams family were held at gunpoint by Baninzi and fellow gang member, Shadrack Nontshongwana, after a family member informed the police of Baninzi's whereabouts. Mrs Adams had pleaded with them to take anything they wanted, but to spare her family's lives. They left with nothing, but returned to shoot each family member in the back of the head.

In addition to his other convictions, Baninzi – along with Nontshongwana – received another four life sentences.

CHAPTER 3

William D. Baker

5 February 2001

Seven years after he was fired by his employer for stealing, 66-year-old William Baker forced his way into the engineering plant where he had worked for 39 years and opened fire with an AK-47, killing five people, including himself, and wounding four others, two critically.

Born in 1934 in Evergreen, Alabama, William Dan Baker had begun working for Navistar International, a major truck- and engine-maker, at their plant in the Melrose Park suburb of Chicago in 1955. He was married at least three times and had several adult children from his first two marriages and a six-year-old son from his latest marriage. He was no stranger to trouble.

In 1993, he pleaded guilty to criminal damage for throwing a bottle through another driver's window on the expressway. The following year, he was fired.

In 1997, he was accused of molesting a 12-year-old girl. When the case came to trial the next year, he pleaded guilty in exchange for prosecutors dropping another charge. He served a month in jail, as well as time on a work-release programme. Put on probation, he was forced to register as a sex offender.

Two weeks before he was convicted, he renewed his Firearms Owner Identification card. His FOID had been issued in February 1993, so he had quite legally purchased the AK-47, a Remington 12-gauge shotgun, a Marlin .30-30 Winchester hunting rifle with scope and the snub-nose .38-calibre police special revolver he later used to kill himself. A .22 calibre rifle was discovered when his home was searched. However, after he was convicted as a felon, his FOID became invalid and he should have surrendered these weapons.

After all these troubles, he separated from his wife. They divorced in the year 2000.

In November that year, along with five other men, he pleaded guilty to playing a role in a scheme to steal $195,400 in truck engines and engine parts from Navistar. He used his forklift to hoist the engines on to a truck driven by another employee.

'Your Honor, I'm sorry I did what I did,' Baker told US District Judge, Harry Leinenweber, at his sentencing. 'I thought I was under the guidance of my supervisor who at the time wanted me to do that.'

Convicted of a second felony, again he should have surrendered his guns.

On 7 November, he was sentenced to five months in prison, to begin in February 2001, followed by five-months' house arrest, and ordered to pay back the $195,400.

The craziness begins

The day before he was due to report to prison to begin his sentence, Baker loaded his arsenal into a golf bag and went to the Navistar plant where he used to work. When a security guard refused him entry, he struck the .38 in her side and forced his way in.

Baker walked through the plant's diesel-engine testing room and sprayed gunfire at workers on his way. His actions were random and not targeted at any specific individuals. Indeed, his victims were all a good deal younger than him and had not been working at the plant when he was there.

After firing 25 to 30 rounds in a span of eight to 12 minutes, Baker walked into a corner office, shot and killed his last victim, and then shot himself in the head with the handgun.

Martin Reutimann, a 24-year-old engineer, was sitting at his desk when he heard gunfire about 10am. At first, he couldn't believe it.

'I heard somebody yell: "There's a guy in the center aisle with a gun!"' Reutimann said, referring to the long hallway where engines are tested. Reutimann said he saw people running past him. He grabbed his coat and cell phone and fled, then called the police.

Bryan Snyder, a 26-year-old development engineer who had worked at Navistar for more than two years, said that he thought at first the attack was a prank.

'It was completely unreal,' he said.

When co-worker Carl Swanson fell to the floor, Snyder said he thought his colleague was playing around. Then, two shots whizzed by Snyder, and a third tore through his upper arm. Forty-five-year-old Swanson was shot in the chest but survived.

Wes Terry, another engineer at the plant, said he saw a co-worker with blood stains on his shirt being helped by another employee.

Fuel systems engineer Robert Jones, a 32-year veteran just 14 days from retirement, knew four of the victims personally.

'I was one aisle away, and I heard shots. It didn't sound like engine noise,' he said. 'I was concerned for my life and wanted to get out of the building as soon as possible.'

Julio Negron, a shipping department worker on disability, came to the plant when he heard the news.

'I said to myself: how could it be Baker? He's such a nice guy,' he said.

It could have been so much worse.

'He had quite a lot of ammunition in the form of clips, boxes of ammunition and loose ammunition,' said Melrose Park Police Chief, Vito Scavo.

The plant employed about 1,400 people.

CHAPTER 4

Dipendra Bir Bikram Shah Dev

1 June 2001

Despite the bloodthirsty history of many monarchies, it is unusual for a member of a royal family to turn into a psycho killer. But perhaps someone should have seen it coming. The pampered Crown Prince of Nepal, Dipendra Bir Bikram Shah Dev, was a heavy drinker and, according to a report on the incident, smoked 'a special kind of cigarette prepared with a mixture of hashish and another unnamed black substance' – probably opium. He had also accumulated an arsenal of weapons that he used to shoot cats.

Things came to a head on the evening of 1 June 2001, when the Nepalese royal family were holding one of their regular monthly get-togethers at the Narayanhiti Palace in Kathmandu. As was the custom, the only people in attendance were royals. No servants or bodyguards were allowed. The 29-year-old Prince Dipendra offered to pour the drinks, though he was already unsteady on his feet after drinking one or two large pegs of Famous Grouse whisky neat. The Queen Mother was with her friends in the sitting room, while the younger crowd hung out around the bar and CD player in the billiards room.

As the evening drew on, Crown Prince Dipendra got so drunk that he was 'stammering and falling down', according to Rajiv Raj Shahi, son-in-law of King Birendra's brother, Dhirendra. The Crown Prince 'misbehaved' with a guest and was told to leave the party by his father, the king. Shahi, along with Dipendra's brothers, Paras and Niranjan, escorted him to his room where he could be heard retching in the en-suite bathroom. He made several loud phone calls. His voice was slurred.

The king must die

Despite the drunken behaviour of his son, King Birendra was in good humour. Drinking a Coca-Cola, he was enjoying the court gossip and became involved in a conversation about gout, uric acid and cholesterol. After about an hour, Dipendra returned to the billiards room dressed in combat fatigues. He was carrying a Heckler & Koch MP5K, a compact automatic submachine gun used by the SAS. Dipendra fired a single shot into the ceiling before turning the gun on King Birendra.

'Dipendra just looked at his father. He said nothing and squeezed the trigger once,' said Ravi Shumshere Rana, Dipendra's 77-year-old uncle, who was standing next to the king when he was shot.

Nepalese Crown Prince Dipendra Bir Bikram Shah Dev killed the entire royal family.

'I instinctively plugged my ears with my fingers and closed my eyes,' recalled Maheshwar Kumar Singh, another of the king's brothers-in-law. Opening his eyes, he found the king 'had a very strange look on his face, and then he began to lean to the right.'

'The king stood there for a few seconds after the firing and then slowly he sat down on the ground,' Rana recalled. Blood appeared on the king's right shoulder and began to spread. 'It was about this time that the King finally spoke. He said: "*Kay gardeko*?" [What have you done?]'

Shahi was a military doctor and ran to the king, pressing his coat to his neck to staunch the bleeding. The king said he had also been shot in the stomach. According to Shahi, Dipendra shot his father and an aunt several times during the carnage.

Prince Dhirendra tried stopping the Crown Prince but was shot in the chest at point-blank range. At that point, Dipendra went wild, raking the room with indiscriminate gunfire. Then, the Crown Prince left the room, only to return with an M16 assault rifle. This time, he shot two uncles and his aunt, among others, and left the room again. He returned several times to finish the job.

Back for more

On one occasion, Shahi had to jump sideways as Dipendra veered towards him, then he managed to escape through a window and told courtiers to call for ambulances. Despite the confusion, there was no doubt who the perpetrator was. Maheshwar Prasad Singh, who saved himself by diving for cover during the shooting, said: 'I'm very sorry to say this, but it was done by Dipendra.'

'What motivated him to do this I am not sure,' said Shahi. 'Had it not been for Prince Paras, probably there would not have been so many survivors.'

Prince Paras had been in a corner of the billiards room, in front of a group of princesses. Eyewitnesses said that Paras saved at least three members of the royal family, including two children, by pulling a sofa over them. When Dipendra returned after a minute, he strode up to the five wounded or dead relatives, including the king, and fired at them again, at point-blank range, and then targeted his sister, Shruti, as she bent over her injured husband. The final time he returned, he pumped bullets into those he had already shot. Then, Dipendra turned his gun toward Paras. Paras shouted: '*Nai*, *Dai! Nai*, *Dai*! [No, Brother! No, Brother!]' He didn't fire.

Dipendra then went out to the garden where his mother, Queen Aishwarya, and Prince Niranjan confronted him. Dipendra shot them both dead, this time with a shotgun. The incident ended when Dipendra shot himself with a pistol on a small bridge over a stream running through the palace. He died in hospital three days later. He had killed nine members of the royal family, not including himself.

The boy who had everything

No one could figure out why he had done it. Everything a prince of the royal line could expect had been lavished on him. Born on 27 June 1971, Dipendra was declared heir apparent to the throne of Nepal the following year. He received his early education at Budhanilkantha School in Kathmandu. He then went to Eton College in England, where he was disciplined for selling alcohol.

After Eton, Dipendra attended Tribhuvan University in Nepal and later joined the Military Academy, Kharipati. He studied for his master's degree at Tribhuvan University and was a PhD student there, too.

In 1990, he became colonel-in-chief of the Royal Nepal Army. He was also patron of the National Sports Council, Royal Nepal Golf Club and Nepal Olympics Committee. He was known to have been skilled in karate and wrote poetry.

At first, the Nepalese government claimed that the shooting was an accident. The late king's younger brother, Prince Gyanendra, who was appointed regent, issued a statement through the official media. It read: 'According to the information received by us, members of the royal family were seriously injured in an accidental firing from an automatic weapon.'

Few believed that so many could have been killed in an accidental shooting. Rumours began circulating that the Crown Prince Dipendra had shot the victims during a family dinner at the palace after a row over his choice of bride. He wanted to marry 22-year-old Devyani Rana, who was half-Indian, but his mother, Queen Aishwarya, was firmly opposed to this.

However, neither Shahi, Singh nor Rana saw any indication of a family row before the incident, which might have set Dipendra off. Later, Paras said that there was another factor involved. The Crown Prince was frustrated that his father had rejected a planned arms deal, which Dipendra had hoped would earn him about $1 million in kickbacks.

'His father, His Majesty, did not agree,' said Paras. 'I know that they argued over it. Dipendra was frustrated. He wasn't happy. He told me. That, to me, was the real trigger.'

According to Paras, Dipendra planned to use the money to elope with Devyani Rana.

'I think he was already making plans for the possibility that he would have to leave the country suddenly if things didn't work out for him. I think this was his back-up plan,' Paras said.

While in a coma, Dipendra was proclaimed king. He reigned for just three days. After he died, Gyanendra, who then took over the throne, confirmed that Dipendra was responsible for the massacre though, under the constitution, he could not have been charged with murder had he survived. A full investigation by two Supreme Court judges also found that Dipendra, alone, was responsible.

End of a dynasty

However, some thought that Gyanendra was behind the massacre because he wanted to seize power. While everyone from Dipendra's family was killed, no one in Gyanendra's was. He had been out of town during the massacre, though his wife and son were present and had been injured. Gyanendra was left as Birendra's closest surviving relative. Conspiracy theorists also claim that Dipendra was right-handed and the gunshot wound that killed him was to the left side of his head.

Those killed by Prince Dipendra were his father and mother, HM King Birendra and Queen Aishwarya; HRH Prince (later HM King) Dipendra himself; his brother HRH Prince Nirajan; his sister, HRH Princess Shruti; (HRH Prince) Dhirendra, King Birendra's brother, who had renounced his title; HRH Princess Jayanti, King Birendra's cousin; Princess Shanti, King Birendra's sister; Princess Sharada, King Birendra's sister; and Kumar Khadga, Princess Sharada's husband

The wounded were HRH Princess Shova, King Birendra's sister; Kumar Gorakh, Princess Shruti's husband; HRH Princess Komal, Prince (now former king) Gyanendra's wife and former queen; Ketaki Chester, King Birendra's cousin and HRH Prince Paras, Crown Prince, son of Gyanendra.

As king, Gyanendra dismissed the government and assumed full executive powers in an attempt to quash the Maoist guerrillas who had taken over much of the country. However, the confrontation soon reached a stalemate. The Maoists declared a unilateral ceasefire in September 2005. Under pressure from the movement for democracy, King Gyanendra agreed to cede sovereign power to the people. The newly constituted House of Representatives declared Nepal a republic and Gyanendra was deposed. On 28 May 2008, the Maoists formed a coalition government and gave the king 15 days to vacate the Narayanhiti Palace, now a museum, and the reign of the Shah dynasty ended after nearly 450 years.

CHAPTER 5

Robert Steinhäuser

26 April 2002

On 26 April 2002, 19-year-old Robert Steinhäuser armed himself with a 9mm Glock 17 and a 12-gauge, pump-action shotgun, and returned to the Johann Gutenberg school in Erfurt, Germany, which had expelled him two months earlier. He went into the lavatory to change into a black combat outfit and a 'ninja-style' mask.

Around 11.05am, he came out with his guns hidden beneath a long black coat, reminiscent of the so-called Trenchcoat Mafia killers, Eric Harris and Dylan Klebold, who murdered 12 students and teachers at Columbine High School in Littleton, Colorado, in April 1999.

He made his way to Room 209, where a maths exam was under way.

Juliane Blank, who was in the classroom, said: 'He must have opened the door without being heard.'

Steinhäuser crept in and sat at the back. When the teacher told students to turn over their papers, he suddenly leapt to his feet, saying: 'I'm not going to take this test.'

That's when the shooting started.

He moved from classroom to classroom shooting the teachers. However, two students were also killed when he fired through a locked door.

'We were sitting in class doing our work and we heard a shooting sound,' said pupil, Filip Niemann. 'We joked about it and the teacher smiled.

'The teacher let us go out and see what was happening and, when we left the classroom, three to four metres in front of us there was a masked person in black holding his gun to his shoulder. He stretched out his gun and fired. We saw a teacher fall to the ground. We just turned and ran. I heard from other kids that the gunman opened classroom doors and aimed at teachers. Even if I believed in God, I would not believe in Him anymore. How could He let something like this happen? What I have seen today will stay with me for the rest of my life.'

No way out

Melanie Steinbrück, age 13, sobbed: 'I heard shooting and thought it was a joke. Then I saw a teacher dead in the hallway and a gunman in black carrying a weapon.'

Juliane Blank, also 13, said: 'The guy was dressed all in black – gloves, cap, everything was black. We ran out into the hallways. We just wanted to get out.'

A girl classmate added: 'He came after us and shot a teacher next to me. He looked deep into my eyes.'

Klare Uhse, 14, said: 'It was a nightmare – first the shots, then the moans of people being hit. I was under my desk all the time, pushed into a corner and hidden by a bookshelf. I could hear people in the classroom tap-tap-tapping messages on to their mobiles. No one wanted to speak in case he came in and shot us too.'

A terrified 13-year-old texted her mum, telling her to call the cops. Another hung a scrawled poster at a classroom window, saying '*Hilfe*' – German for 'Help'.

German radio played a frantic mobile phone call made by a child to her mother: 'We're all crammed into one room. The teacher's one of the dead. Everyone's crying.'

At one stage, Steinhäuser was holding 28 pupils hostage in a classroom. Many of the school's 800 students fled the buildings in terror as he ran amok. Some hid in storerooms and lockers to escape the madman.

Survivor Kerstin Gübler, 17, said: 'I saw him in the corridor. All I could see were burning eyes, bulging eyes aflame with hatred.'

Another pupil named Felix said: 'At the end of our lesson, three pupils went out and came back in with shocked faces saying: "This can't be true."

I followed them and around the corner was one of my teachers lying on the floor. At first, I didn't realize what was going on and I walked up to him and said to the others: "This is just a joke." I felt his pulse and tried to talk to him, but he wasn't there anymore. It looked unreal. A second teacher was also lying dying nearby and pupils tried to help him. He was still shaking. Shots followed and somebody said: "Get out, get out." I grabbed my rucksack and ran out.'

Help arrives

When the police turned up at about 11.10am, Steinhäuser shot an officer in the head, killing him. Fighting back tears, Erfurt police chief, Rainer Gruber, later told reporters: 'It was his daughter's birthday today.'

Steinhäuser's rampage was halted by 60-year-old history teacher, Rainer Heise. He had been supervising an art class when he heard a loud bang.

'It sounded as though chairs were being thrown around,' he said. At first, he thought that there had been an accident in the chemistry laboratory.

As he left his classroom, he saw students running along the school corridors. Suddenly, he was face to face with a man clad in black who was shooting in the air. Then the gunman shouted: 'Damn, I've got to reload,' and pulled out some bullets from a pocket in his pants.

As the gunman was reloading his pistol, Heise ran to the school secretariat. The door was locked, but he shouted and banged on it. After a moment, the school principal opened and let him in.

'There are dead people here,' she told Heise in a trembling voice.

As he entered, he saw the assistant principal sitting at her desk – shot dead. The school secretary was lying on the floor. She, too, had been killed.

Heise told the principal that he would check to see if all students had escaped from the school building. He left the secretariat to look into the classrooms on that floor. From the window of the art room, he shouted to the police below: 'We need four ambulances. The gunman is still in the building.'

The police told Heise to keep away from the window. He hid in the art cupboard. After a while, he heard a noise outside and thought that it might be a student trying to hide somewhere, so he opened the door and peeped out – only to be confronted by the gunman, pointing his gun directly at him. Heise grabbed him by the shirt and tried to talk to him.

'Then, all of a sudden, he takes off his face mask,' Heise said. The teacher realized the gunman was his former student, Robert Steinhäuser.

'I ask him: Robert, what's all this about? Was that you shooting?' Then Heise said: 'If you're going to kill me, go ahead and shoot me, but look me in the face.'

Steinhäuser dropped the gun and replied: 'No, Herr Heise. That's enough for today.'

Heise pushed him into a room and locked the door. Shortly afterwards, Steinhäuser shot himself. By then, he had killed 16 people. The police found the body surrounded by a pool of blood, with another 500 bullets by his side. Heise said he did not know why he had survived. 'Perhaps he just liked me. Perhaps he didn't think I was bad.'

During his 20-minute frenzy, Steinhäuser had fired 40 rounds from the Glock pistol, but had not used the shotgun. The son of middle-class parents, he was welcome at the local gun club and was carrying both guns legally. He owned two others. He also had 1,200 rounds of ammunition and the police suspected he had been planning the attack for some time.

Bloodbath

The alarm had been raised by a caretaker. Minutes later, a special forces squad surrounded the school. Commandos combed the building and found the grisly scene of the massacre on the first floor.

Housewife Gerda Puhlmann, who lived nearby, said: 'The sky was filled with helicopters and there were armoured cars on the street.'

She revealed that she asked a cop what was happening. He replied: 'Madame, it's a massacre.'

Rainer Gruber, president of the Erfurt police, said: 'When the special troops arrived, they systematically searched the building and found a picture of horror – corpses in the corridors, in the classrooms and in the lavatory.'

Some were so badly mutilated that medics could not tell whether the dead were men or women. One cop told reporters: 'It was truly a bloodbath because blood was flowing down the corridors like water spilled from a bucket.'

'Many of the victims were killed with headshots. He clearly was a trained marksman,' said Bernhard Vogel, premier of the state of Thuringia, whose capital is Erfurt.

A police spokesman said: 'The gunman shot people one by one. It was an incredibly cruel and calculating execution of innocent people. Teachers were the main target and the two pupils who died probably just got in his way.'

Outside, cops urged parents to register their children's names before going home. Dazed students huddled in the street, hugging and crying.

So why did he do it? Steinhäuser boasted about devil worship. In computer chatrooms, Steinhäuser sometimes signed off as 'Son of Satan'. But this did not convince.

'There is little evidence so far that he is a so-called Satanist,' one police officer said, 'but we are following up the available clues.'

A compact disc found in Steinhäuser's room called 'School Wars' contained the line: 'Shoot down your naughty teachers with a pump gun.'

Though Steinhäuser was carrying a pump-action shotgun, he used a pistol for the fatal shootings.

Otherwise, any psychological abnormalities were difficult to spot. He had posters of Victoria Beckham rather than Adolf Hitler on his bedroom wall. The police removed a collection of violence-laden comics and computer games that featured 'intensive weapons usage'. Steinhäuser's mother told police she had not noticed any unusual behaviour in her son, though he had few close friends.

'Robert was a troubled youth, but it was a trouble that he largely masked,' said Erich Sixtmann, a friend of his father. 'He was rude with teachers, got reports on his card like "doesn't respond to discipline well". But he wasn't a kid who pulled the wings off butterflies or tortured cats. He became introverted from about the age of 12. He liked military things and collected a lot of books on the war. I don't think it was a Hitler worship thing, but who knows now.

'In the gun club, he found an acceptance that I think he found hard to get in everyday social contact. He didn't have a girlfriend, for example, and took to dressing in black and hanging out with "gothic-dressing" friends. He was in search of who he really was. Had he been booted out of school and given some counselling, then this might not have happened. But he wasn't and it did. He was immature and lashed out. This was some terrible revenge, the motive for which was buried deep beneath a benign, outwardly peaceful exterior.'

Ticking timebomb

In the weeks leading up to his expulsion, he forged sick notes and spent his days on the range at the local gun club. His expulsion, which he kept secret from his parents, was the culmination of an uneasy relationship between Steinhäuser and his school. On a school field trip to Berlin, he staged the mock execution of a teacher.

'He pretended to make a pistol out of his hand and was full of hatred as he took aim at the teacher. The teacher was extremely angry. Robert got a reprimand for that. He said he was just fooling around,' said Cassandra Mehlhorn, 19.

Mr Heise also recalled the incident. He said that fellow teacher, Hans Lippe, had caught Steinhäuser smoking a cigar. Steinhäuser had then pulled his hands from his pockets, pretending that they were pistols with his thumbs as triggers.

'The student was drunk,' said Heise. 'He walked towards Mr Lippe and, with the cigar hanging from his mouth, he pointed the fingers at him and said: "Rat-a-tat-a-tat-a-tat, you're dead."'

'I never thought of him as a person capable of something like this,' 18-year-old Thomas Rethfeldt said. 'Some say he was picked on, but if he was it wasn't much. He was reserved. I never thought he was a person capable of violence. He was actually rather intelligent, but he didn't seem to care very much about school. There was nothing at all out of the ordinary about him.'

One psychiatrist told a local television station in Thuringia: 'He was a timebomb all right. Some release the pressure through love or sex or drink, but sometimes the pressure is too great. Jeffrey Dahmer, the cannibal killer, gave into it in the end. Charlie Manson, the boys who ran amok at Columbine... there is a broad belief for disaffected youth that there is something almost erotic, something sexy, about death and destruction. Unformed minds seize on to this like a limpet. He was such a limpet.'

Former classmate, Isabelle Hartung, 18, said: 'The crime just doesn't fit him at all. He was a funny guy who liked his life.'

He had so much to live for.

'He had good grades,' she said. Marks were not the reason he was expelled and the school was known for its academic record, sending many students to the universities of Heidelberg and Göttingen.

Hartung added: 'He once told me he wanted to be famous and known to everyone. Now, when I think back to what he said, it really freaks me out.'

Behind the mask

One teacher described the former student on German television as a calm and reserved person.

'He never seemed to seek any conflict,' Claudia Hickl, a friend of his mother, said. 'Robert was tightly wound up, you could see that. He was polite, but I often wondered what was behind that politeness. He was looking for love I think and was deeply disturbed when his parents split up when he was just 11 or 12.

'His mother told me once she thought about getting him counselling but hoped he would "grow out" of his moods. Some days, he would not talk to her for hours on end, just sitting in his room playing heavy metal records over and over. He was a boy who demanded attention. Perhaps he should have received it.'

It was later discovered that he was a member of the sinister Blue Rose Cult – an internet-based ring of lonely and delinquent youngsters, who are into Gothic music and devil worship. The cult had been linked to at least 15 teenage suicides in eastern Germany in the previous two years, and there have been reports that some members slaughtered animals as part of satanic ceremonies.

Others take part in bizarre rituals where they slash each other with razors and then drink the blood of their friends. The group encourages teenagers to talk about their miserable lives and useless existences in chatrooms. It is a fine blend of alienation, existential teenage angst and a numbed fascination with ultra-violence and the dark side.

Via email, members of the Blue Rose Cult even encourage each other to commit suicide. In November 2000, an 18-year-old from Klietz in Germany jumped out of a window to his death. On his computer were messages from the Blue Rose Cult telling him to take his own life.

CHAPTER 6

Derrick Todd Lee

1998–2003

Although he had a rap sheet that extended back to 1993, the first-known victim of Derrick Todd Lee, aka the Baton Rouge Serial Killer, was Gina Wilson Green, a 41-year-old nurse and office manager. A divorcee, she lived alone in a block on Stanford Avenue in Baton Rouge, near Louisiana State University. Her body was found in her apartment on 23 September 2001. She had been sexually assaulted and strangled. Her purse was missing, along with her Nokia cell phone. This was later found in an alleyway on the other side of town.

Eight months later, there was another murder in the vicinity of LSU. On 31 May 2002, the body of 22-year-old Charlotte Murray Pace, a graduate student, was found by her roommate at a townhouse on Sharlo Avenue less than 3 km (2 miles) away. Death was due to stab wounds, but she, too, had been sexually assaulted. A strange coincidence linked the two killings. Charlotte Pace had moved to Sharlo Avenue only two days before. Previously, she had lived just three doors away from Gina Green, although there was no evidence that they ever knew each other.

Again, items were missing. The killer had taken the keys to Charlotte's BMW along with a tan and brown Louis Vuitton wallet that contained her driver's licence. A silver ring had been stolen and, again, her cell phone was missing. However, her assailant left behind a clue in the form of a footprint. It had been made by a man's Rawlings brand trainer, size ten or 11. Unfortunately, it was a brand found widely in discount stores.

The attacks continue

On 12 July 2002, 44-year-old Pam Kinamore went missing. She was an antiques dealer who ran her own business in Denham Springs, a few kilometres east of

Baton Rouge. It was a Friday evening and she shut up shop as usual, before driving home to 8338 Briarwood Place in Baton Rouge itself.

Her husband arrived home later to find his wife's car in the driveway, but she was nowhere to be found. The evening passed with no sign of her, so he eventually phoned the police. Four days later, her naked body was found in a boggy area of woodland under the Whiskey Bay Bridge in Iberville Parish between Baton Rouge and Lafayette.

A postmortem revealed that she had been sexually assaulted. The cause of death was a stab wound to the neck. Again, things were missing. The killer had taken a silver toe ring from her body. The police quickly tied her murder to those of Gina Green and Charlotte Pace – and another case.

Two days after Pam Kinamore had gone missing, a 28-year-old Mississippi woman was raped by a man who had forced her into a white pick-up on Interstate 10, which runs westwards from Baton Rouge to Lafayette. After the assault, he had let her go and she gave the police a good enough description of her attacker for them to put together a composite.

Then, a week after Pam Kinamore's body had been found, a woman came forward claiming that she had seen a woman answering Kinamore's description slumped in the passenger seat of a white pick-up truck the night she had gone missing. She appeared to be sleeping or was, perhaps, dead. The truck had been speeding westwards down I-10 at around three o'clock in the morning. It had turned off at the Whiskey Bay exit, the ramp nearest to where Pam Kinamore's body was found. The driver was a white male, who, the witness said, had a slight build. This was surely the same man as the mystery rapist.

The police now put together a detailed description of the vehicle. When DNA evidence confirmed the connection of the murder of Pan Kinamore to those of Gina Green and Charlotte Pace, a multi-agency murder task force was formed. They knew a serial killer was on the loose.

DNA evidence linked the murders of Gina Green and Charlotte Pace. Later, the Louisiana State Crime Lab managed to show that Kinamore had been killed by the same man. Now certain that they had a serial killer on the loose, the police began combing through unsolved homicides over the last ten years.

On 21 November 2002, 23-year-old Trineisha Dene Colomb had disappeared. At around half-past-one in the afternoon, her black 1994 Mazda MX3 was found on Robbie Road in the small town of Grand Coteau, 80 km (50 miles) west of Baton Rouge and some 19 km (12 miles) north of Layafette. The keys were still in the ignition, but Colomb was nowhere to be seen. Her naked body was found three days later by a rabbit-hunter in a wood 48 km (30 miles) away. Colomb was a US Marine and fought back before she was bludgeoned to death. DNA evidence soon linked Colomb's killer with the Green, Pace and Kinamore murders.

There were other similarities to the earlier murders. Another footprint was found, again of a man's athletic shoe in size ten or 11. CNN identified it as the latest model of a $40 Adidas-style basketball shoe widely on sale in the area. And some of the victim's possessions were missing, including a ring with the word 'Love' inscribed on it. But there were some unique features. This was the first time the killer had struck outside Baton Rouge itself and Trineisha Colomb was thought to be the Baton Rouge Serial Killer's first-known Black victim.

On the day Trineisha went missing, a white pick-up truck was seen in the same wooded area where her body was found. The driver was described as around 35 years old and white, and investigators released a new composite showing 'a person of interest'. Meanwhile, DNA samples were collected from 600 volunteers. Mouth swabs were taken from another 100 potential suspects the following month.

With the growing publicity surrounding the Baton Rouge Serial Killer, enrolment in self-defence classes soared, along with sales of guns and pepper spray. Attendance at Louisiana State also climbed, with students turning up to class rather than staying at home where they feared being abducted and murdered.

Lights on, nobody home

In March 2003, the Baton Rouge Serial Killer struck again. The next victim was Carrie Lynn Yoder, a 26-year-old, post-graduate student at Louisiana State. She lived alone at 4250 Dodson Avenue, not far from Charlotte Pace and Gina Green. On 3 March, she told Lee Stanton, her boyfriend of three years' standing, that she was going to the Winn Dixie grocery store on Burbank Drive. They arranged to talk again later that night or the following day. When she did not call, he began to worry. On 4 March, he drove by her house and noted that the lights were on and her car was outside, but he left it at that. The next day, he went back to the house. The back door was open and he went in. Her keys, purse and cell phone were on the counter. Everything else seemed to be in order, except for a wall-mounted key rack near the front door. It was hanging by one screw as if it had been dislodged during an altercation. Stanton called the police.

Searching the house, they found a well-stocked fridge and cupboards, indicating that Carrie Yoder had returned from the store before she went missing. Questionnaires were handed out at the Winn Dixie. Meanwhile, helicopters searched the area.

Ten days after Carrie Yoder went missing, an angler found her body in the Atchafalaya River near the Whiskey Bay Bridge – not far from where Pam Kinamore's body had been dumped eight months before. She had been badly beaten and she had put up a fierce fight before she had been strangled. DNA evidence showed that she was the fifth victim of the Baton Rouge Serial Killer.

On 17 March 2003, the family and friends of the victims staged a demonstration on the steps of the Louisiana state capitol in Baton Rouge. The task force's response was to tell the public to ignore the composites previously circulated. They were now looking for a man of any race or description. Nor should they only be on the lookout for white pick-ups. The killer might be using a vehicle of any type.

The investigation then took a surprising turn on 23 May 2003 when Fox News reported that members of the task force were looking into three

Derrick Todd Lee, the Baton Rouge Serial Killer.

incidents in which a young black man attacked women in St Martin Parish, though none of them were killed. A composite was produced, showing a light-skinned, African American male who, initially, tried to charm his victims. Until then, it was assumed that the Baton Rouge Serial Killer was white.

On 5 May, DNA swabs had been taken from a man who resembled the composite and were sent to the crime labs for analysis. They matched the DNA taken from the body of Carrie Yoder and three more victims of the Baton Rouge Serial Killer.

The DNA belonged to 34-year-old Derrick Todd Lee, who lived in St Francisville in West Feliciana Parish, 32 km (20 miles) north of Baton Rouge. He had given the sample voluntarily nearly three weeks earlier, but later that day his wife, Jacqueline Denise Lee, took their two children out of school, saying the family were moving to Los Angeles. Packing up their belongings, they fled, first to Chicago, then on to Atlanta.

The harm behind the charm

On 27 May, he was arrested in a tyre store in Atlanta. For a week, he had been living in Lakewood Motor Lodge, where other residents found him to be a 'very nice man', who grilled ribs and chicken at a party and set up a Bible study class. He even charmed a number of women there, inviting them back to his room for a glass of cognac. Lee waived extradition proceedings and was flown back to Louisiana voluntarily the next day. Initially, he was charged with the murder of Carrie Yoder. However, by early June, he was also charged with the rape and murder of Gina Green, Charlotte Pace, Pam Kinamore and Trineisha Colomb.

Lee had a criminal record that stretched back to 1984 when he was caught peeping into the window of a St Francisville woman's home at the age of 15. He had a string of arrests for peeping and stalking, as well as for illegal entry, burglary, assault and resisting arrest, that continued until 1999. Then, things got more serious.

In January 2000, he was accused of attempted murder after severely kicking his girlfriend, Consandra Green, after an argument over Lee's advances towards another woman in a bar. While fleeing the police, he tried to run over the sheriff's deputy and got two years. After being released the following year, he was arrested for wife-beating, but the charges were dropped. It was said that his wife 'lived in denial of her husband's transgressions, which included stalking, peeping into windows and infidelity'. At one point, against his wife's wishes, he moved a mistress into the family home. The police in Zachary, Louisiana, 16 km (10 miles) north of Baton Rouge, also suspected Lee of the murder of 41-year-old Connie Warner in 1992 and the disappearance of 20-year-old Randi Mebruer in 1998.

His name was also linked to the murder of Lillian Robinson, a 52-year-old prostitute from St Martin Parish between Lafayette and Baton Rouge, whose naked body had been found in the Atchafalaya River, near Whiskey Bay Bridge, on 10 February 2002. She had gone missing the previous month. Her body had been in the water for more than a week and was so badly decomposed it was impossible to obtain reliable DNA samples.

Lee was also a suspect in the disappearance of Melinda McGhee, a 31-year-old mother of two, who disappeared from her home in Atmore, Alabama, on 24 March 2003. Although Melinda McGhee's home was some 354 km (220 miles) from Baton Rouge, it was easy to get to up the interstate and there were striking similarities between McGhee's disappearance and those of Kinamore and Yoder. However, no body had been found.

Possibly, another woman had fallen victim to the Baton Rouge Serial Killer in May 2002, when the car of Christine Moore, a 23-year-old student at Louisiana State, was found abandoned near River Road in Baton Rouge. She had left home to go jogging in a park, but never returned. Her body was found on a dirt road in Iberville Parish in June. Like Trineisha Colomb, she had been bludgeoned to death. Despite its similarities to the other killings, her death was not formally attributed to the Baton Rouge Serial Killer.

The police were particularly eager to trace Lee's wife, Jacqueline. She was found by the FBI in Chicago in June, with the couple's two children. They had received an anonymous tip-off that more bodies had been buried under a concrete slab at the couple's home and needed her consent to dig it up.

They also set about excavating the driveway at the former home of Lee's girlfriend, Consandra Green, as Lee had been seen pouring concrete to form a roadway there in the middle of the night only a couple days after Randi Mebruer had disappeared from her home in Zachary, Louisiana, in 1998. A woman's bracelet was found, but the search for human remains drew a blank at both of the sites. However, in February, DNA evidence linked Lee to Randi Mebruer's disappearance. The police in Bolton, Mississippi, also tried to tie Lee to the slaying of four women found near a truck stop as he had once been a truck driver.

Investigators were still puzzled by the white pick-up seen in the Kinamore murders. They impounded a truck from Consandra Green's uncle, said to have been sold to him by Lee, but no connection was ever established between it and the murders. As the witness had said that the driver of the truck was white, the pick-up she had seen might have had nothing to do with the murders. Then, there was the rape victim who had been sexually assaulted by a white man in a white van.

The verdict

On 24 September 2003, Lee was formally indicted with the first-degree murder of Trineisha Dene Colomb of Lafayette, Louisiana. However, the district attorney decided not to take that case to trial. The following Wednesday, Lee was charged with the attempted rape and murder of Diane Alexander, a nurse in Breaux Bridge outside Lafayette. She claimed that Lee had beaten her and attempted to rape and strangle her in her trailer in 2002 – and would have succeeded if her son had not come home and scared him off.

Lee was also charged with the murder of 21-year-old Geralyn DeSoto, who was found beaten and stabbed in her mobile home at Addis, across the Mississippi from Baton Rouge, on 12 January 2002 – the day she registered as a graduate student at Louisiana State. This was a second-degree murder charge because the prosecution felt it could not prove an underlying felony, such as forced entry or rape, which is needed for the charge of first-degree murder in Louisiana.

Lee was found guilty of the second-degree murder of Geralyn DeSoto on 10 August 2004, after his 15-year-old son testified to seeing his father's bloody boots. The verdict brought a mandatory life sentence. On 12 October, Lee was found guilty of the first-degree murder of Charlotte Murray Pace after the prosecution was allowed to introduce evidence from other suspected Baton Rouge Serial Killer cases to prove a pattern. As he was taken from the courtroom Lee shouted: 'God don't sleep.' Then, he cried: 'They don't want to tell you about the DNA they took eight times.'

While he was found guilty in these two cases, he was not prosecuted in any of the others. No one has explained the discrepancies between the person of Derrick Todd Lee and the serial-killer profile – or even in the early evidence. Nevertheless, he was sentenced to death by lethal injection, but died quietly in hospital of heart disease in 2016 before the sentence could be carried out.

CHAPTER 7

Levi Bellfield

2002–2004

On 23 June 2011, Levi Bellfield was found guilty of the murder of 13-year-old Milly Dowler, who went missing on her way home from school in Weybridge, Surrey, on 21 March 2002. Her remains were found in Yateley Heath Woods, Hampshire, on 18 September 2002.

Milly was seen walking down Station Avenue, but she did not appear on CCTV farther down the road. However, the camera did catch Bellfield's girlfriend's red Daewoo Nexia minutes after Milly was last seen. Bellfield admitted driving the car. Attention turned to Bellfield after he was convicted of the murder of 19-year-old Marsha McDonnell and 22-year-old Amélie Delagrange as well as the attempted murder of Kate Sheedy, then 18, in the same area of west London where Milly went missing.

Born in Isleworth, west London, in 1968, Bellfield was a bodybuilder and worked as a nightclub bouncer and as the manager of a car-clamping company. He was convicted of assaulting a police officer in 1990 and had multiple convictions for theft and driving offences.

He also considered himself God's gift to women, siring 11 children with five different partners. During his trial, the prosecution alleged that he stalked women in the streets and talked to them at bus stops. He attacked those who rejected him. He was thought to have been responsible for 20 attacks in all.

Detective Sergeant Jo Brunt spoke to several of his ex-girlfriends.

'He was lovely at first, charming, then completely controlling and evil. They all said the same,' said DS Brunt.

Control freak

Within a couple of weeks of meeting them, Bellfield would take their mobile phone and swap it for another, which contained only his number, saying it was all they needed.

He would then stop them from seeing friends, parents or going out without his permission, and would constantly phone to check what they were doing. Following an argument, one girlfriend said he told her to sit on a stool in the kitchen and not move. He went to bed and she sat there all night.

'We asked her what she did about going to the toilet and she said she would rather wet herself than move from that stool,' said DS Brunt. 'That shows how frightened they were of him.'

Detective Chief Inspector Colin Sutton, who led the murder hunt, characterized Bellfield as 'a psychology PhD waiting to happen'.

'When we started dealing with him, he came across as very jokey, like he's your best mate,' said DCI Sutton. 'But he's a cunning individual, violent. He can switch from being nice to being nasty, instantly.'

DCI Sutton explained his own theory. 'He has a massive ego to feed; he thinks he's God's gift to everyone. He drives around in his car, feels a bit "whatever" and sees some young blonde girl.'

According to his last girlfriend, Emma Mills, Bellfield always chased after small blonde girls with large breasts. It was no coincidence all his victims were of a similar appearance.

'Young blonde girl says: "Go away," and he thinks: "You dare to turn down Levi Bellfield, you're worth nothing" – and then she gets a whack over the head,' said DCI Sutton. 'It is shown in the case of Kate Sheedy. She was smart enough to think she didn't like the look of his car and crosses the road. He thinks: "You think you're so clever," and whoosh, he runs her over.'

What's more, he reversed over her when she was on the ground.

Kate was the head girl at her convent school in Isleworth at the time of the attack in May 2004. She had spent the evening saying goodbye to friends after her last day at Gumley House School and was walking home when she was mown down.

She had organized celebrations for the sixth form leavers and gave a speech remembering her time at the school. Because of the attack, she missed her A-levels but was granted her predicted grades, AAB, by the exam board and went on to study History and Drama at York University, though one year later than she had hoped. Even so, she remained mentally and physically scarred by the attack.

In a statement, she said: 'On the day I was attacked, I was celebrating moving on to a new and exciting time in my life. All that hope and excitement was taken from me and I thought my life had changed for ever. I will never be able to forget what happened to me, the scars on my body and the memories I have are something I will never be rid of, but hopefully I can move on.'

On top of the physical and mental ordeal, there was also additional trauma and stress from the police investigation.

Search for victims

While he was under police surveillance, Bellfield was seen driving around in his van, talking to young girls at bus stops. It is thought that he must have spotted Amélie Delagrange getting off a bus in August 2004. CCTV cameras recorded her walking towards Twickenham Green after she missed her stop on the bus home. She slowed her pace between the last two sightings, around the time Bellfield passed her in his van.

DCI Sutton said she probably stopped to speak to him. Minutes later, she lay dying from massive head wounds in the middle of a cricket pitch.

Amélie had come from Amiens in France to study English and worked in a patisserie in Richmond. She had a close circle of friends, both English and French. Her parents travelled from France to attend the trial at the Old Bailey. The couple said Bellfield had shown an 'unbelievable level of arrogance' and had winked and mouthed obscenities to family members during the proceedings.

Levi Bellfield found fame as the killer of Milly Dowler and others.

Marsha McDonnell was bludgeoned to death just metres from her front door in Hampton after she got off a bus in February 2003. Described in court as an 'attractive blonde', she was on a gap year before starting university, but still lived at home with her parents, two sisters and a younger brother. She was passionate about music and a music room at the local children's hospice is dedicated to her memory.

The jury of seven women and five men was unable to reach verdicts on two other charges. These were the kidnap and false imprisonment of Anna-Maria Rennie, 17, and the attempted murder of hairdresser, Irma Dragoshi, 33.

DCI Sutton said: 'We looked at a dozen crimes in west London and we have not been able to eliminate Levi from any of them. I fear we may have only scratched the surface.'

Bellfield was sentenced twice to life imprisonment. On both occasions, he was given a whole life order, the first person in England to receive two life orders. While in jail, he was granted permission to marry after appealing under the European Convention on Human Rights at a cost of up to £30,000 in legal aid, according to the *Daily Mail.* Meanwhile, a book claimed that he was having sex with a female prison officer in Wakefield Prison. She was sacked and the wedding was cancelled.

CHAPTER 8

Sean Vincent Gillis

1994-2004

For Sean Gillis, murder was a game. After being arrested in April 2004, he told FBI agents that he was playing chess with them as they investigated his crime scenes. He said he used television news to predict his next move and to judge whether he was winning.

'I was the chess master, then,' he said. 'You're not going to beat me. My basic interest would be, "Okay, did they find it? Where did they find it? What was the condition of the body?"'

Gillis had always been a great fan of murder. On the internet, he graduated from watching porn to crime-scene sites that showed the bodies of dead women. When the police searched his home, they found computer files entitled *Best of Snuff*, *Beheadings and Hangings* and *Manson Murders* about Charles Manson who terrorized Los Angeles in 1969. The subject of another file was necrophilia in Russia. Several books about serial killers, both fiction and non-fiction, were also seized from his home, along with a 'murder and mutilation' kit that included plastic zip ties, a machete, several knives and eight saws, along with photographs of his victims.

He closely followed the murderous career of his rival, Derrick Todd Lee, who was also operating in the Baton Rouge area. There was a file on his computer titled *DTL* and he kept a newspaper cutting about Lee's last victim, Carrie Lynn Yoder. While Lee was in custody, Gillis continued killing, so in the press he became 'The Other Baton Rouge Serial Killer'.

Daddy was a psycho

Born in 1962, Gillis was said to have been an exemplary child until, one day, his mother returned home to find his alcoholic father holding a gun to the boy's head and threatening to kill them both. Disarmed, he was remanded to a mental hospital.

Although his father was out of the picture, his mother took him to see his paternal grandparents regularly and he had a good relationship with them. While his mother described him as a normal boy, he gave the other kids in the neighbourhood 'the willies'. She insisted he was very well behaved and only spanked him once, with a belt, and regretted it.

At school, he made good friends. In their adolescence, his gang began smoking marijuana and became interested in Satanism. He enjoyed having a secret life, hidden from his doting mom. But others noticed disturbing signs. Neighbour Carolyn Clay recalled: 'About three in the morning, I awoke to a loud noise coming from their yard. Sean was in the front yard beating wildly on some garbage cans. He told another neighbour that he was frustrated because he didn't have a girlfriend. He was prone to fits of anger like that. He was an angry young boy.'

His mother did not see that side of him. At 17, he was reunited with his father and was disturbed to discover that he was a homosexual. He was horrified by his dad's collection of gay pornography. He, therefore, refused to visit him in his new home in California. Soon he began to build a rap sheet of minor crimes.

Home alone

In 1992, his mother took a job with a TV company in Atlanta, Georgia, but Gillis refused to accompany her and stayed behind in their house in Baton Rouge. Neighbours again remarked on his peculiar behaviour. He was seen in the garden on all fours, howling at the moon, and was found peeping into a local lady's house, pretending to be looking for his cat. The police were called.

Terri Lemoine, who worked in a local convenience store, knew nothing of this. She was attracted to him, though she found him a little nerdy, if harmless. She decided that, if she was going to have a serious relationship with him, she must put him to the test. One day, during an argument, she seized the chance to slap his face. With tears in his eyes, he insisted that violence should play no part in their relationship. He had no such reservations outside it.

Around this time, Gillis broke into a nearby retirement home in the early hours of 21 March 1994 with the intention of raping 82-year-old Ann Bryan. When she started screaming, he cut her throat with the foot-long hunting knife he habitually carried around. While she was bleeding to death, he stabbed her 47 times in the face, then began slashing her breasts, body and genitals. The nurse, who came to give her her medication the next morning, found her nearly decapitated and disembowelled.

When Lemoine moved in with Gillis, she discovered that he was addicted to pornography and was appalled when he tried to show her websites featuring the victims of sex killers. What she did not know was that, when she was out working at night, he was cruising Baton Rouge's rough north side, looking for women.

On 4 January 1999, he picked up 30-year-old African American prostitute, Katherine Hall. Once she was in his car, he lassoed her with a plastic cable tie, choked her, stabbed her in the throat and the left eye, stripped her, had sex with her corpse, mutilated her and dumped her bloody body in plain sight under a Dead End sign.

Asked why it had taken him five years to kill a second time, he said it was because he had been happy.

Acts of evil

Four months later, he spotted 52-year-old mother of three, Hardee Moseley Schmidt, out for a morning jog in a well-heeled neighbourhood on the south side of Baton Rouge and began stalking her. It would be three weeks before he pounced.

At 6.30am on Sunday 30 May, he ran into her with his car and knocked her into a ditch. With a cable-tie around her neck, he dragged her into his car, drove her to an isolated spot, raped her, killed her and mutilated her body, which he loaded into the trunk of his car.

When he went to pick up Lemoine from work, she said she noticed a funny smell. Gillis said that he had run over a squirrel and would wash the car. Later, he dumped Hardee Schmidt's naked body in a bayou next to the highway, 56 km (35 miles) from Baton Rouge, where it was spotted by a cyclist the next day.

On 12 November 1999, Gillis picked up 36-year-old Joyce Williams in the Scotlandville district of Baton Rouge, took her across the Mississippi and strangled her in a cane field near Port Allen. He took her body home to dismember it, eating some of the skin and her severed nipples. He said he liked the look of her legs, so he cut one of them off and kept it.

Sean Vincent Gillis played murder as a game.

When he picked up Terri Lemoine from work, the remains of Joyce Williams' body were hidden on the back seat. The next day, he dumped her dismembered corpse in a sugarcane field across the river near Port Allen.

Though he liked to dump his victims' bodies in plain sight, Williams' corpse was not found until January 2000. That same month, he killed 52-year-old Lillian Robinson. He did not have time to mutilate the body before Terri finished work, but he toyed with it and put his penis in her mouth. Again, her naked body was dumped in a bayou, where it was found by an angler a month later.

In late October 2000, he was visiting his god-daughter in Lafayette when he spotted 38-year-old prostitute, Marilyn Nevils. After picking her up, he strangled her, took her body home and had a shower with it. He then dumped her body by a levee on the banks of the Mississippi, 5 km (3 miles) from his home, where the decomposing corpse was found on Halloween. It was not identified.

Gillis then took a break from killing for more than a year, though his interest had not diminished as he followed the activities of Derrick Todd Lee, who he feared might outdo him.

Meanwhile, Gillis renewed his friendship with 45-year-old divorcee, Johnnie Mae Williams, and her three children. Ten years earlier, she had been the cleaner at the Gillis house. Now, she was a crackhead and supported her habit by prostitution. It is rare for a serial killer to kill someone they know, but in October 2003 he drove her to a secluded area, beat her, raped her and murdered her, cutting off her hands. Then he posed for photos with her mutilated body, leaving it exposed on top of a bank.

On 26 February 2004, Gillis picked up 43-year-old prostitute, Donna Bennett Johnston. She, too, was a mother and crack addict. That night, she was drunk and in no state to put up any resistance. They were near his home when he strangled her, before going about his butchery. He slashed her breasts and cut off a nipple, which he ate. He excised a tattoo as a souvenir, then cut off her left arm at the elbow. It is thought that he took this home with him to use the hand to masturbate. He took 50 photographs of her body, then took it to another location where he left it in an obscene pose.

God-hater

With Derrick Todd Lee now firmly under lock and key, the police formed a new task force to hunt The Other Baton Rouge Killer. When dumping two of his victims, he had left tyre tracks. With the help of Goodyear, the police were able to identify the tyre and got a list of everyone in Baton Rouge who bought them. DNA swabs were taken from everyone on that list, including Gillis. When his matched samples from the crime scenes, Gillis was arrested at home in front of Terri Lemoine, who insisted that they had got the wrong man.

'Don't you realize that you are living with a serial killer?' a policeman asked.

She could not believe that the man she had taken to be a mild-mannered nerd had killed eight women until he admitted it. All Gillis could find to say to Terri was 'sorry'.

Along with the DNA evidence and the murder kit they took from the house, the police also had written evidence. Gillis had written to Tammie Purpera, a friend of Donna Johnston's who was dying of AIDS, saying: 'Your friend died quickly. She was so far gone that night that I really do not think she even knew what was happening to her. She was so drunk it only took about a minute and a half to succumb to unconsciousness and then death. Honestly, her last words were, "I can't breathe." I still puzzle over the post-mortem dismemberment and cutting. There must be something deep in my subconscious that really needs that kind of macabre action.'

Otherwise, he said he really didn't 'know what the hell is wrong with me… I was in a real bad place. I was pure evil that night. No love, no compassion, no faith, no mercy, no hope.' He blamed his actions on his lack of faith, saying that he had 'hated God for a long time'.

In August 2007, he pleaded guilty to the second-degree murder of Joyce Williams and was sentenced to life. In July 2008, he was found guilty of the murder of Donna Johnston and was sentenced to life without parole after the jury was deadlocked over the death penalty. On 17 February 2009, Gillis also pleaded guilty to the murder of Marilyn Nevils and was given another life sentence. When she had disappeared in Lafayette, no one reported it and the Baton Rouge police did not even know she was missing until Gillis admitted murdering her.

CHAPTER 9

Mohammed Bijeh

March–September 2004

Mohammed Bijeh and his accomplice Ali Baghi were dubbed 'hyenas' or 'vampires of the Tehran desert' in the Iranian press. They were convicted of raping and killing 17 boys between the ages of eight and 15, two men and a woman in the desert south of Tehran.

The men lured children into the desert by saying they were going to dig out rabbits or foxes from their burrows. They then stunned their victims with blows from a stone, sexually abused them and buried the bodies in shallow graves, placing dead animals near their victims' bodies to cover up the smell of the rotting corpses.

Reports indicated that the pair picked some of their victims from poor Afghan families, refugees who may have been living in Iran illegally, so some of the disappearances were never mentioned to police.

It was also reported that the father of one of the victims complained that Baghi had been let out on bail at one point. He also alleged that the two men were merely a part of a larger group 'dealing in children's body parts'.

'We are ready to pay the judiciary as much as they want, so they can hand them over to us and we can deal with them,' the man said.

The case drew huge media attention, with one reader writing to a newspaper asking for the alleged killers to be burned alive in a brick furnace. President Mohammad Khatami ordered his interior minister to investigate the case personally.

After confessing in court, 23-year-old Bijeh was tied to an iron pole and given 100 lashes on his bare back, while a crowd of 5,000 chanted 'harder, harder'. He was stabbed by the brother of one of the victims, who had evaded security, and fell to his knees three times during the punishment. Then, the

Mohammed Bijeh, vampire of the Tehran desert.

mother of another victim was invited to put the noose around his neck. Bijeh was hoisted some 10 m (33 ft) in the air by a crane. This was a cruel and lengthy form of death as it did not break the neck. It is a common form of execution in Iran.

The crowd applauded. Some people burst into tears, crying out the names of their injured children. Others shouted: 'Shame on you, Bijeh!'

After about 20 minutes, the body was lowered and a doctor confirmed Bijeh was dead.

Baghi was also flogged and sentenced to 15 years in jail.

CHAPTER 10

Terry Blair

2–4 September 2004

In 2008, 47-year-old Terry Blair was convicted of the murder of six women in Kansas City four years earlier. Two other murder charges were dropped, along with three rapes and one assault. At the time of the crimes, he had been paroled after serving 21 years of a 25-year sentence for the murder of his pregnant girlfriend, Angela Monroe, the mother of his two children, in 1982. According to court records, he was angry with her for performing acts of prostitution.

Blair was the fourth child of ten and raised in poverty. His mother, Janice Blair, had shot and killed a man in 1978, but was sentenced to probation after making an Alford plea – that is, pleading guilty while maintaining your innocence in order to receive a lesser sentence. She went no further in school than ninth grade and suffered from mental illness. Her sentence was seen as unduly light. As a condition of parole, she was directed to receive outpatient counselling, therapy and psychiatric treatment.

The following year, her son, Walter Blair Jr, was charged with murder. He had met a man in jail who offered him $6,000 to kill 21-year-old Katherine Jo Allen before she could testify against him in a rape trial. Walter Blair confessed to abducting Allen from her apartment, taking her to a vacant lot and shooting her as she begged for her life. Blair later recanted and there were doubts about the credibility of the state's chief witness. Nevertheless, he was executed in 1993.

Another of Janice Blair's children, Clifford Miller, was sentenced the following year to two life terms, plus 240 years, for kidnap and forced sodomy. In 1992, he had abducted a woman from a bar. After shooting the woman in the arm, prosecutors said Miller drove her to an abandoned house where he raped her and beat her until she passed out. She was hospitalized for more than two months to recover from the gunshot wound, a fractured skull, a broken jaw and smashed cheekbones. Almost a year later, a friend persuaded the victim to go back to the bar where she recognized her attacker and Miller was arrested.

Anonymous tip-off

On 3 September 2001, a caller dialled 911 and told the dispatcher that he wanted to report a dead body. He told them precisely where the body could be found.

'How do you know a dead body is there?' the dispatcher asked.

'I put it there,' the caller said.

When asked to give his name, the caller, said, 'Oh, no,' and then repeated where the body was.

'Look up under the branches under the bushes by the alley,' he said. 'It's an abandoned house. It's red.' He said the body had been there for two months.

When asked if he knew the victim's name, he said he didn't.

'She's a prostitute,' he said. 'So were the other two.'

'You killed them also?' he was asked.

'Yeah.'

The dispatcher asked how he killed them, suggesting: 'You strangled her?'

The caller then hung up.

In the second call the following day, the caller said he wanted to report two more bodies of prostitutes. He called them 'scum'.

'It's a disgrace,' he said. One of the bodies had been there a week and was starting to stink. He refused to give his name, but said he could be referred to as 'Scott' and that he would call again the next day. He said there were six more bodies to be found.

Police arrested Terry Blair within weeks of the calls after his DNA matched semen in and on victim, Sheliah McKinzie, 38. During more than

11 hours of interrogation, Blair denied knowing McKinzie or having sex with her and confessed to nothing. On 15 October 2004, Blair was charged with her murder. Bail was set at $500,000. Prosecutors pointed out that this was irrelevant because, even if Blair made bond, he would remain in jail for violating parole in the previous homicide case. On 3 December, the other charges were added. This time, bail was refused.

Blair waived his right to a jury trial in exchange for the prosecution not seeking the death sentence.

Who was on the phone?

Thomas Purnell, an assistant professor of linguistics at the University of Wisconsin-Madison, testified for the defence.

'It's unlikely that the two speakers, the 911-call speaker and Mr Blair, are the same person,' Purnell said.

In his testimony, Purnell described the complex analysis he performed on the 911 calls alongside telephone conversations between Blair and his grandmother and Blair and a television reporter that were made while Blair was in jail awaiting trial.

Purnell said Blair and the caller shared some voice characteristics, such as being male, urban and an African American raised in the United States. But, he said, among other things, their pitch and pacing were different.

On cross-examination, Assistant Prosecutor Michael Hunt asked Purnell if the caller could have been disguising his voice because 'he's talking to police and telling them about six people he's killed'.

'When he's talking to his grandma, the consequences are a whole lot different than when he's talking to the police about six murders he committed,' Hunt said.

Purnell said the caller could have been disguising his voice and acknowledged that he had never performed such an analysis before for court proceedings. He had only done them in the classroom.

Hatred of women

A former prostitute told police that, before the 911 calls, Blair had said he was killing all the prostitutes one by one. The mother of one victim said she last saw her alive when she dropped her daughter off to meet Blair and two other men. And a teenage witness testified that Blair told her that whoever was killing the women probably had a good reason.

The only other evidence linking Blair to the murders was the semen found on Sheliah McKinzie's body. But the defence argued that hairs and DNA also left links to others.

'Some of this DNA is not his,' defence attorney Cynthia Dryden said. 'When you start pulling out one part and considering only some… you can make it fit whatever you want.'

The presence of his semen, she maintained, showed only that he had sex with her, not that he had killed her. But Jackson County Circuit Judge, John R O'Malley, concluded that the placement of semen indicated McKinzie hadn't moved or attempted to clean herself after having sex.

'Since we know this semen belonged to Mr Blair we must conclude he was present as Ms McKinzie expired, her throat crushed by his hands and by his irrational, evil hatred of women,' he said.

If Blair had killed Sheliah McKinzie then, it followed that he had killed the other women the 911-caller had admitted killing, giving details that only the killer could have known. Blair was convicted of six murders and sentenced to life in prison without possibility of parole on each.

Professor of Criminology, Steve Egger, was not surprised, given Blair's family history of violence.

'Once you have someone socialized into a culture of violence,' he said, 'they learn to express themselves in a violent manner and it becomes second nature.'

CHAPTER 11

Carl 'Charlie' Brandt

15 September 2004

Thirty-seven-year-old TV executive, Michelle Jones, invited her aunt Teri Brandt and uncle Charlie to stay with her in Orlando for the weekend when Hurricane Ivan threatened their home on the Florida Keys. She was close to both of them, particularly Teri, who was just eight years older than her, and was delighted when they accepted.

'Twenty minutes after they got there, I got the phone call from Michelle. "Teri and Charlie are here, where are you? Why aren't you over here?"' said Michelle's friend, Lisa Emmons. 'They were hanging out.'

Lisa and other friends often hung out at Michelle's home, which had a Jacuzzi and a pool.

Michelle's mother, Mary Lou, who lived in North Carolina, phoned to find out how the weekend had gone. She and her daughter were close and spoke on the phone almost every day, so she was puzzled when she did not answer.

'We placed a call to Michelle Monday night and Tuesday night. We got her voice mail,' Mary Lou recalled. By Wednesday night, when there was still no answer, Mary Lou was beginning to worry.

She called Debbie Knight, another close friend of Michelle's, and asked her to go check on Michelle. She stayed on the phone while Debbie walked up the drive to Michelle's home.

Debbie then found that the key Michelle had given her wouldn't open the front door, so she went around to the garage.

'There was a garage door with almost all glass, so you could see in,' Debbie said. 'I was in shock.'

Grisly sight

Inside the garage, she could see Charlie hanging from a rafter. He was suspended by a bedsheet around his neck and a ladder was nearby. It looked like he had committed suicide.

There were more gruesome scenes inside the house. Deputy Rob Hemmert, lead investigator for Florida's Seminole County Sheriff's Office, found Teri slumped on a sofa. She had been stabbed seven times in the chest.

Michelle was found in her bedroom. She had been decapitated. Her heart, liver and left leg had been removed, and her body surgically dissected.

All three bodies were locked inside the house. There was no indication of any type of struggle or fight. That led the investigator to one inescapable conclusion: that 47-year-old Brandt had committed the murders and then hanged himself.

Everything seemed fine

There had been no indication that anything like this would happen. Friends who spoke to Teri said that everything seemed fine. That weekend, Charlie took the opportunity to visit his father, Herbert Brandt, who lived in nearby Ormond Beach. He told investigators that, as his son was leaving: 'Charlie hugged me like he's never hugged me before.'

Then, Deputy Hemmert pieced the events of their last evening together. Things seemed to have started innocently enough.

'I know they had dinner together. Charlie cooked some type of fish. It looks like they may have had some drinks, some wine and so forth,' he said.

After dinner, Michelle called Lisa, warning her not to come over.

'She said Teri and Charlie had been arguing and they weren't the best of company. They had a little too much to drink. She was tired and she wanted to go to sleep,' Lisa recalled.

It seems that the Brandts had planned to leave that day as their bags sat in the front hall. But Charlie had insisted on staying an extra night.

'There was no reason for them to stay behind,' Hemmert said. 'The hurricane had passed, so he chose to stay for a reason. I think that was because he knew what he was going to do.'

Brandt used Michelle's own kitchen knives to kill both her and his wife.

'Teri was killed in a quick, repeated stabbing-type attack to her chest,' said Hemmert. 'In comparison, Michelle had one stab wound to the chest.'

He then carefully put her blood-soaked clothes in the bathroom sink, before dismembering Michelle's body.

'It all took time. And it took thought,' said Hemmert.

When he was finished, Brandt changed his clothes, leaving his bloody ones on the floor by the bed. He left behind something else that puzzled the investigators – Victoria's Secret bras and underwear, cut in half, were scattered around the room.

Then Brandt walked into the garage and climbed a stepladder. He tied a bedsheet around his neck and hanged himself.

Mary Lou couldn't accept that this monstrous crime was the work of the mild-mannered brother-in-law she had known for 17 years.

'When they described what had happened to Michelle, it was even beyond description,' says Mary Lou.

The crime was just as incomprehensible to Michelle's horrified friends, who considered Charlie, a bit of an oddball but certainly no threat.

'He was just very quiet and reserved,' Lisa remembered. 'He would just sit back and observe. Michelle and I used to call him eccentric.'

But Charlie was well suited to Teri's carefree personality, according to Debbie. 'Teri was gypsy-like. Just happy-go-lucky. Nothing bothered her. She was a wonderful person. Very kind, very sweet,' she said.

Teri's closest friend, Melanie Fecher, said Teri and Charlie were inseparable. 'If my husband could love me one-third the amount that Charlie loved Teri, I'd be the luckiest woman in the whole world,' she said.

Melanie said she never saw any problems in Teri's marriage. They never argued. She never saw him get angry and she said, to her knowledge, Charlie didn't even have a temper.

Everyone agreed that it had seemed a perfect match. 'They often did things for each other that would make each other feel good,' said Hemmert. 'One of those things was that they would make their lunches for each other. Because the lunch tasted better when it was made by the one who loved you.'

Nevertheless, Charlie stabbed his wife seven times and left no note or explanation.

Family secret

A clue came from Charlie's older sister Angela. She had been invited to attend a briefing by the police but stayed in her car in the parking lot outside. Afterwards, she talked to Deputy Hemmert and revealed a family secret that had been kept for three decades.

Back then, when Angela was 15 and Charlie was 13, they had lived with their parents and two younger sisters in Fort Wayne, Indiana. Just after 9pm on 3 January 1971, Angela was reading in her room.

'My mom was in a bath and my dad was shaving. And I heard my father yell: "Charlie, don't" or "Charlie, stop!"' Angela told Hemmert.

Charlie walked into a bathroom while his father was shaving and shot him in the back, hitting him three times as he went down. Charlie then stood over the bathtub where his mother was bathing and fired several rounds into her body, killing her. She was eight months pregnant at the time.

'The last thing I remember hearing my mom say was "Angela, call the police,"' she told Hemmert in the taped interview.

But Angela didn't get the chance. After shooting their mother, Charlie had turned the gun on her, but it wouldn't fire and they started fighting. Angela said that she tried to calm Charlie down by telling him how much she loved him.

'I saw the madness, the glazed-over look. I saw it disappear,' Angela said.

Dressed only in a bloody, torn nightdress, Angela ran screaming out of the house. She fled through a snowstorm to a neighbour's house and pounded on the front door. By the time 16-year-old Sandi Radcliffe answered, Angela had fled to the next house and Charlie was outside instead.

'There was just a "knock, knock" and I opened up the door and he goes: "Sandi, I just shot my mom and dad,"' she said.

Momma's boy

At the time, this was reported as a freakish crime by a quiet kid – the last kid on earth, friends said, who would shoot anyone, much less kill his mother.

'That's why this whole incident was such a shock because they were very close, incredibly so. He was a momma's boy,' said Sandi.

Another neighbour said: 'He used to baby-sit constantly with those two younger daughters.' She recalled how he would ride them around on his bike, 'just doing what he was supposed to do'.

Detective Dan Figel went to the hospital to interview the critically wounded father.

'He just kept saying: "I don't know why my son did this. I have no idea as to why my son did this,"' Figel recalled.

Ronald Pancner was one of three psychiatrists who examined Charlie.

'Basically, I was looking for mental illness. And he wasn't showing the signs and symptoms of serious mental illness, which I thought was what the court wanted to know,' said Pancner. 'This kid did well in school. He didn't get into any trouble. He loved his family, he said. And the family said that he was a loving kid, you know. So, there wasn't anything to diagnose.'

But there had to be something wrong with him.

'To the layperson, this doesn't make sense. The guy killed his mother. She's pregnant. Shot his father. Why doesn't he have a mental illness? But he doesn't have a diagnosable mental illness,' Pancner said. 'We found no psychosis, no distorted thinking that would basically be a reason for this crime to be done.'

Asked why Charlie turned violent, Pancner said: 'We don't know.'

In court, asked why he had done it, Charlie told the judge: 'I didn't really want to. It was like I was sort of programed. I hesitated, but the next thing I knew I had shot them.'

There was only one theory. The family had just returned from a quail-hunting trip to Florida, where their father had used a gun to put down their ailing dog.

A six-person grand jury that reviewed the shooting in May 1971 determined that the boy was not criminally responsible. Under Indiana law at the time, it was deemed that children under the age of 14 could not understand the consequences of their actions. The grand jury recommended that he receive psychiatric treatment, adding that 'it is possible that such antisocial conduct could repeat itself in the future'.

Charlie was sent to a psychiatric hospital, where he stayed just over a year when his forgiving father, who had survived, won his release. Herbert Brandt then pulled up stakes and moved the family to Florida.

'He never spoke to Charlie about what took place,' says Hemmert. 'Never said: "Hey, Charlie, why did you shoot me? Why did you kill your mother?" You know? "What were you thinking? How about an apology?" None of those things. He just accepted him back into the home as if nothing happened.'

Even Charlie's two baby sisters, too young at the time to remember the incident, were never told the truth about their mother's death.

Herbert Brandt remarried and returned to Indiana with his two youngest daughters, though he settled back in Ormond Beach when he retired. Meanwhile, Charlie remained in Florida, where he met and married Teresa Helfrich and moved out to Big Pine Key. He got a job as a radar technician with Lockheed Martin Corp., working on Fat Albert, a surveillance blimp tethered at Cudjoe Key.

Madness in his method

Thirty years had gone by between the murder of his mother and that of his wife and niece. Hemmet was sure that, if he looked hard enough, he would find evidence that Brandt was a serial killer. He had travelled widely around the United States and abroad. The authorities in Germany and The Netherlands contacted Seminole County Sheriff's Office.

Criminal profiler Leslie D'Ambrosia, who had analyzed dozens of cold cases, said: 'There's no boilerplate profile for a – quote – serial killer. It doesn't exist. It's all individual; it's based on a person's life experiences and everyone has a different life experience.'

It was noted that Brandt was precise and methodical.

'How a person normally behaves is translated into how they carry their crimes out,' says D'Ambrosia. 'He's quite organized and planned in what he does. He's intelligent, very reliable, very responsible.'

The Brandts' house on Big Pine Key had been boarded up meticulously in preparation for the storm.

'I'd never seen anything like it,' said Hemmert. 'Charlie took it to the extreme. Every piece of wooden panel that was cut for each window looked like it had been custom-fit. The holes for the doorknobs on the French doors were meticulously cut. Perfectly round circles.'

Inside the house, things were just as precise. On the back of the bedroom door, there was an anatomical poster of a female, the sort you would see in a doctor's surgery.

'Charlie and Teri were not in the medical profession. We saw no reason for that chart to be there. What is this doing in someone's home?' said Hemmert. 'Her hair's put up in a bun. Which I had never seen before. And it's showing the skeletal system and the muscular system.'

Teri would have seen the poster every day and Hemmert wondered whether she hadn't considered it a big deal. It certainly made him suspicious.

'I'm looking at a chart that's got these portions of the body exposed. And he's virtually duplicated or exposed some of those areas of the body in what he did with Michelle,' Hemmert said.

Investigators also found medical books, journals and an anatomy book. 'And, in that book, there was a newspaper clipping that showed a human heart,' said Hemmert. 'Knowing what he did to Michelle and then finding those things, it all started to make sense.'

There were also Victoria's Secret catalogues in the house, addressed to Charlie.

'He always referred to Michelle as "Victoria's Secret". He gave her that name. And he never referred to her as Michelle,' said Hemmert. A colleague at work told him that Brandt often talked about his niece and what a beautiful woman she was. He didn't know his niece's name as Brandt referred to her only as 'Victoria's Secret'.

Far from being just a friendly uncle, Brandt had been secretly infatuated with his own niece.

'He was fascinated by her, and I think ultimately he intended killing her,' said Hemmert. 'I think that's evident in the way he spoke about her and the things that he looked at on the internet.'

When investigators examined Brandt's computer, they found he had been on websites that featured death fantasies, necrophilia and violence against women with names such as 'erotic horror', 'death fetish erotica' and 'drop dead gorgeous'.

A computer expert recovered information that investigators think Brandt erased, probably to conceal it from his wife.

'It's like peering into his mind and seeing what he was thinking,' said Sheriff Don Eslinger. 'You see disembowelment, you see decapitation and dead women.'

'You saw where he may have gotten some of his ideas and thoughts and fantasies from,' said Hemmert. 'The thing that we noted immediately was that the things he did with her body did not appear to be someone who had done this for the first time – there had to be more.'

More victims?

An FBI computer program selected the 26 slayings in Florida as the focus of the investigation, some simply because the victims were young women, but many because there were unusual aspects to the slaying, such as mutilation. Add to that almost 400 cases of missing women while Brandt was in the state.

'A lot of these cases are cold cases. They're old. They may not have the physical evidence,' Hemmert said. 'They require an enormous amount of time and legwork. And the resources are limited everywhere. But we're not going to give up.'

D'Ambrosia didn't think we would ever know how many murders Brandt was responsible for. But three jumped out. In 1978, 12-year-old Carol Lynn Sullivan disappeared from her school bus stop in Osteen, 48 km (30 miles) from Ormond Beach when Brandt lived there. Only her skull was recovered, found along a wooded roadside in nearby Deltona inside a rusted paint can.

Then there was the 1995 murder of Darlene Toler, a prostitute in Miami's Little Havana. Her body was found alongside a highway. She had been decapitated and her heart had been removed.

'The body was wrapped up in a blanket, then wrapped up in plastic and tied, almost like a package,' explained detective, Pat Diaz, who handled the investigation. Dog hairs were found in the blanket. The police also found dog hairs in the back of Brandt's truck. The truck also yielded another clue.

'Every time he put gas in the truck, he kept the mileage,' said Diaz. In those mileage records, a spike occurs right around the time Toler was killed, 160 km (100 miles) away from Brandt's home.

Asked whether he thought Brandt drove from the Keys to Miami just looking for somebody, Diaz said: 'He had come to Miami. He and his wife worked opposite shifts. And he did what he had to do.'

DNA analysis of animal hair is difficult and costly, but police said that – if they got it – a match would close the Toler case.

'That'll get me to 100 per cent. It wouldn't be 99, it'd be 100 per cent,' said Diaz.

Then there was another murder closer to home. In July 1989, local fishermen found a woman's body under a bridge off Big Pine Key, just four blocks from the Brandts' home. She was 38-year-old former beauty queen, Sherry Perisho, who had fallen on hard times and lived on a dinghy. As with the other victims, Perisho was decapitated, her heart cut out. There were cut marks to the bottom of the dinghy, which the police think Brandt used as a dissection table. For years, all investigators had to go on was a sketch of a man spotted running across the highway near the scene.

The question is: did Teri know what her husband was up to? Michelle's parents, Mary Lou and Bill, were sure that Charlie had never told his wife that he'd killed his mother.

'I don't think she would have married him, period, at all had she known,' explained Bill. They said that Herbert and Angela Brandt never acknowledged that telling Teri might have saved lives. Mary Lou said Herbert and Angela should have known that Charlie had the potential and capacity to kill. She added that Herbert never made any effort 'to say how sorry he was that this happened to us'.

However, Angela's ex-husband, musician Jim Graves, who had introduced Teri to Brandt, believed that she did know. Angela had told him some time earlier.

'I came home one day and she was crying rather uncontrollably, and said she had something that she absolutely had to talk to me about,' Jim recalled. But, after getting to know him, he agreed that Charlie had put the past behind him and was now okay.

'He was so gentle that, when there was a bug in the house, he would refuse to step on it and carried it outside,' Graves said.

But then, one day, after he and Angela split up, the two men got to talking.

'We were havin' a few beers after fishing all day and everything,' said Graves. 'I was just really despondent. Somehow, we started talking about revenge. Well, you know you get your feelings hurt and wanna lash out. I believe he looked at me and said, "Well, if you really wanna get revenge, you should kill somebody and cut their heart out." And it creeped me out at the time.'

Shadows of the past

Graves soon forgot about it. Years later, when his new girlfriend wanted to fix up her friend Teri, Jim called Charlie.

'No way in the world would I know that they would fall in love and get married!' said Graves.

He was best man when Teri and Brandt got married on 29 August 1986.

'I did have a conversation with Charlie. And I insisted that he inform her of his past,' Graves said.

He was sure that Charlie had told Teri about the 1971 shooting.

'After they got married and I went down to visit them I asked them when they were gonna have kids,' he said. 'And she told me, considering everything, that she didn't think it was a good idea.'

Graves took her response to mean that she knew. He had another conversation with Teri after Sherry Perisho had been killed.

'She goes: "Well, you know, somebody was killed not too far from our house. I'm thinkin' about, you know, callin' the sheriff." And I said, "Well, why?" And she goes: "Well, because of Charlie's past,"' Graves recalled.

Shocked, Graves said he later confronted Charlie. 'I looked at him and I said: "You know, your wife thinks you might've committed this heinous act." And he was like, "I didn't do it,"' Graves said.

When investigators were looking again at the Perisho murder, they talked with Graves, who, under oath, was much more specific about Teri's story.

'She apparently found Charlie downstairs and he had blood on him. And she asked him what had happened and he gave an excuse that he was filleting fish, although it was a workday, it was in the evening, she went ahead and believed him,' investigator detective, Trish Dally, recalls. This was enough to close the Perisho case, officially.

One puzzle remains. Why wasn't there any mention of this time in Teri's diaries, which investigators found in their house and which reflected a very ordinary life?

'They weren't detailed writings, they were just something very simple from – went fishing, caught a good bull dolphin, to nice dinner with Charlie. Boat ran out of gas. Buy steaks for dinner,' said Hemmert.

There were few hints of anything wrong.

'We only found a couple of interesting notations and those were "weird day". But there's nothing more specific, and we have no idea what occurred to cause her to write that,' said Hemmert.

Teri also noted times when Charlie was out late, even out all night, but never added explanations in her diary entries. If she suspected that he was continuing his career as a killer, why did she stay with him when it led to her own death and that of her niece?

CHAPTER 12

Juan Manuel Álvarez

26 January 2005

Methamphetamine addict and a man prone to delusional behaviour, Juan Manuel Álvarez parked his gasoline-soaked Jeep Cherokee Sport vehicle on the Metrolink train line in the Glendale suburb of Los Angeles, California. His intention, he said, was to kill himself. At the time, the 25-year-old father of two was experiencing marital difficulties.

But at the very last moment, he changed his mind. As the train approached, he jumped out of the car.

At 6.03am on 26 January 2005, the southbound commuter train hit the SUV and jack-knifed, hitting a stationary Union Pacific freight train in a siding on one side and a northbound Metrolink train on the other. Spilled diesel fuel then caught on fire. The train wreck killed 11 and injured 200.

Later, the police found Álavarez wandering the streets, saying repeatedly: 'I'm sorry.' They arrested him after it was established that it was his vehicle parked on the tracks.

Following an investigation, the police concluded that he had intended to cause the crash without committing suicide and the authorities filed additional charges against him for murder with intent. Prosecutors sought the death penalty for his crimes under a seldom-used law making train wrecking, causing a person's death, a capital offence. This 1873 law was created to prosecute Old West train robbers, who were known to blow up the tracks to rob a train.

Bid for attention

During the eight-week trial, the prosecution argued that Álvarez had intended to kill the commuters as part of a sick attempt to get attention from

The aftermath of the Glendale train crash.

his estranged wife. The defence maintained that the incident was an abortive suicide attempt as Álavarez had slashed his wrists and stabbed himself repeatedly in the chest. However, there was some speculation that Álvarez might have inflicted the wounds on himself after the crash, based on some early reports by witnesses.

'I was going to kill myself,' Álvarez testified. 'I feel terrible and I ask for forgiveness.'

The jury took a day to find Álavez guilty of 11 counts of murder in the first degree and one count of arson. He was acquitted of the train-wrecking charge. At the sentencing hearing, the jury recommended that he serve life imprisonment without the possibility of parole, rather than death, and he was sentenced to 11 consecutive life sentences.

Handing down the sentences, Los Angeles County Superior Court Judge, William R Pounders, said: 'I don't believe for a minute you intended to kill yourself or harm yourself in any way. I think you were setting up a scenario, so you could go back to your family.'

He added that if there was 'a sentence known as forever… I would give it to you' as Álvarez had 'shown no remorse to this court' for his actions.

The defence lodged an appeal on the grounds that the judge erred in excluding expert testimony to show that it was improbable and unforeseeable that a collision between a train and a passenger vehicle would result in derailment, a train-on-train collision and death to a person on a train.

The conviction was upheld and the California Supreme Court refused to review the case. An appeal against the sentence was also denied.

CHAPTER 13

Ronald Dominique

1997–2006

On 1 January 2000, the body of small-time, African American criminal, Michael Rydell Vincent, aka Chris Vincent, was found hanging from a barbed-wire fence on Highway 7 in Lafourche Parish, Louisiana. He had died from asphyxia. There were ligature marks on his wrists, but the autopsy report did not record that he had been raped, though it did note that there were abrasions to his scrotum.

The body had been left there by 35-year-old Ronald Joseph Dominique, who found fame as the Bayou Blue Killer. He had been raping and killing for some time, and was happy to advertise his activities, figuring that he was invincible.

Dominique had been brought up in Thibodaux, the parish seat of Lafourche. At school, he had been ridiculed for being gay, though he had remained firmly in the closet. He claimed that a priest had molested him, but his parents did not believe him. At the age of 21, he pleaded guilty to making obscene phone calls and was fined $74, plus costs. At 30, he was charged with drunken driving. Two years later, a half-naked young man jumped from Dominique's bedroom window, screaming: 'He's trying to kill me.'

The police were called. During the three months Dominique spent in custody awaiting trial, he claimed to have been brutally raped by other prisoners, splitting his anus. This had to be stitched up and left him particularly sensitive in that area. But Dominique got lucky. The young man who had escaped through his bedroom window could not be found and he was released in November 1996. The experience left him determined never to go back to prison, particularly Louisiana's notorious state penitentiary, Angola. Nevertheless, his criminal career continued.

Litany of death

His first murder seems to have been that of David Mitchell, a 19-year-old African American, who had disappeared in nearby St Charles Parish on the outskirts of New Orleans on 13 July 1997. He had been sodomized and drowned, before his body was dumped in nearby Hahnville. On 14 December 1997, the body of 20-year-old African American, Gary Pierre, was found in St Charles Parish. He had been raped and strangled.

Then, on 31 July 1998, 38-year-old Larry Ranson went missing in St Charles Parish and his body was dumped. Again, he had been raped and strangled. As the bodies were found close to one another down the same road, the police figured they were the work of the same killer. But there were no clues to work on – no fingerprints, no hairs or fibres, and no DNA. The rapist-killer had used a condom.

On 3 October 1998, 28-year-old African American hustler, Oliver LeBanks, went to the Rawhide – aka the 'Raw Hole' – a popular gay bar in New Orleans. There, he met Dominique, who was derided as a fat slob and a loser. Nobody liked him – even when he did his Patti LaBelle drag act.

Dominique offered to pay LeBanks for oral sex. They went out to his car. After some mutual fellatio, Dominique sodomized LeBanks. But when LeBanks tried to return the favour, Dominique grabbed a tyre iron and beat his brains out, then strangled him with his belt just to make sure he was dead.

Now with a body to dispose of, Dominique drove out into the suburb of Kenner. He looked for a place quiet enough to dump the body without being caught, but busy enough for the body to be found easily. Reading about the discovery of his victims' bodies in the newspapers was part of the kick.

On the Earhart Expressway, Dominique passed a state trooper and took care to obey the speed limit. Stopping on a deserted freeway ramp, he pushed LeBanks' body out of the passenger door, then dragged it over to the parapet by the belt that was still around its neck and let it drop. The following day, the body was spotted by a passer-by, who reported it to the local sheriff in Jefferson County.

However, with the murder of LeBanks in Jefferson Parish, Dominique had left some clues. There were some tyre prints in the soft sand where he had stopped and there were marks of a ligature around LeBanks' wrists. He had been tied up.

During the postmortem, it was noted that he had Caucasian hairs on his body. These were collected with tweezers and put in a sealed bag, so any DNA would not be contaminated. LeBanks, who had a criminal record of his own, was identified from his fingerprints. Interviews with friends and family led detectives to the Rawhide.

Two weeks after LeBanks was killed, the partially clothed body of 16-year-old African American Joseph Brown turned up in St Charles Parish. A month after that, 18-year-old Bruce Williams' body was dumped in Jefferson. Both had been sodomized and strangled. Like LeBanks, Williams had been a hustler and had gone missing from New Orleans. The FBI were called in. Their profiler concluded that the killer lived near the airport – which narrowed it down to around a million men. But the profiler was right. Dominique lived less than 24 km (15 miles) from New Orleans International (now Louise Armstrong International).

Next, on 30 May 1999, the half-naked body of 21-year-old African American hustler Manuel Reed was found in a dumpster in Kenner, the New Orleans suburb where the airport is situated. He had been raped and strangled.

Another 21-year-old African American hustler, Angel Mejia, went missing on 30 June 1999. His partially clothed body was found abandoned next to a dumpster that night. Once more, he had been sodomized and strangled.

While the corpses rendered few clues, the press got wind of a serial killer on the prowl. On the mistaken idea that all the bodies had been found barefoot, headline writers dubbed him the 'Shoeless Serial Killer'. In fact, some victims were found wearing shoes and, in cases where they weren't, their shoes were usually found nearby.

The corpses pile up

The killer appeared to be goading the police when he dumped the body of a 34-year-old African American, Mitchell Johnson, just metres from where LeBanks had been found. Johnson had last been seen in Kenner on 1 November 1999. A suspicious-looking white guy, in his 30s with puffy cheeks and receding hair, had been seen cruising the area at the time. A sketch of the suspect was drawn up and distributed to both the gay and mainstream media.

After it was published in the *Times-Picayune*, New Orleans' major newspaper, Dominique quit his job and moved the trailer he lived in from Boutte, 24 km (15 miles) west of New Orleans, to Houma, 97 km (60 miles) to the southwest. He parked it in the yard of his sister Lainie's place on Bayou Blue Road. He got a job as a labourer and bought a second trailer, which he parked next to the first. Although Houma was a rundown rural city in the backwoods of Louisiana, it had two gay bars.

After killing Michael Vincent on 1 January 2000, Dominique did not kill again, but he did get in trouble with the police. On 19 May 2000, he pleaded guilty and paid a fine for disturbing the peace to avoid going to court. Then, on 10 February 2002, he was arrested again for slapping a woman in a Mardi Gras parade. Again, he avoided standing trial by signing up for community service.

He took a job as a pizza delivery man with Domino's and spent weekend afternoons calling bingo numbers for senior citizens at the Lions Club. However, preparing to resume his career as a serial killer, he towed one of his trailers out to a remote spot in the bayous.

Dominique's next victim was a serial sex offender himself. Kenneth Fitzgerald Randolph Jr, a 20-year-old African American and near neighbour of Dominique, had been arrested three times for having sex with a minor. Although he had a felony conviction, he was on parole, when his body, naked except for his socks, was found in the cane fields on 6 October 2002. There were ligature marks around his wrists and throat.

On the evening of 12 October 2002, small-time criminal Anoka 'Noka' T Jones told his girlfriend he was going out to smoke a cigarette. The next morning his partially clad body was found in Dominique's old stamping ground of Boutte. He was identified by his fingerprints and an autopsy concluded he had been raped and strangled with a ligature.

The police interviewed his friends and criminal associates, some of whom he owed money to. A couple were picked up on suspicion but released when the links between the Jones and the Randolph killings were noted. Again, it appeared that a serial killer was at work.

On 24 May 2003, two young men out dirt-track riding found the body of a Black man, partially stripped, in a cane field outside Houma. Fingerprints identified him as teenager Datrell Woods, who had repeatedly been in trouble with the law. It was clear he had been dumped there. There was no dirt on the soles of his socks and his bicycle, abandoned nearby, had no dirt on the tyres – nor were there any tyre tracks. However, the previous day, a witness had seen a white or cream-coloured car coming down the dirt road in the cane field. It had turned on to Highway 56.

Interviews with Datrell's family and friends led nowhere. Soon, it became clear that he was another victim of the serial killer in the area. However, Dominique took another break from murder and was careful not to attract attention. Meanwhile, he took a job as a meter-reader, which made him familiar with the backroads.

Under cover of Tropical Storm Matthew, which struck the Louisiana coast on 10 October 2004, Dominique dumped the body of another Black male near a pond 32 km (20 miles) away in the Des Allemands area. Fingerprints identified him as Larry Matthews, a drug dealer from Thibodaux. Again, there were signs that he had been strangled, though he may also have overdosed with cocaine. The rain from the tropical storm had washed any other clues away.

Soon afterwards, the naked body of a middle-aged man was found in a storage unit. None of the 50 people who rented other units at Gator Storage had noticed anything out of the ordinary. The *Houma Daily Courier* quickly linked this corpse with the others. A dragon tattoo on his arm identified the deceased as Michael Barnett. Dental records confirmed this. What made him different from the other victims was that he was white.

On 20 February 2005, more dirt-track riders came across a body near the small airport the oil companies used outside Houma. The detective who came to the scene recognized the victim as Leon Lirette, a friend of Noka Jones. He had been very drunk when he was strangled. A white guy with a maroon car was seen near where the body had been dumped.

Another body was found in a wood in Lafourche Parish on 9 April 2005. The victim was identified as 32-year-old African American, August Terrell Watkins, from Houma. He was homeless after being forced to move out by his former girlfriend, Elizabeth Jones. She said that a white man in a white truck had been looking for Terrell. His brother said that the white man was a friend of Terrell. Jones also said that she had later seen Terrell's new girlfriend, Winter Lewis, in the white truck with the white man. But this line of investigation went nowhere.

Eaten by rats

Up until that point, the state of Louisiana's resources had been used to track down Derrick Todd Lee, aka the Baton Rouge Serial Killer. A Black man killing white women commanded media attention; a white man killing mainly Black, gay men did not – even though his body count was more than double. Nevertheless, with bodies spread over the jurisdiction of four parishes, the authorities finally agreed to form a task force in March 2005. Fourteen cops drawn from the parishes, the state and the FBI were put on the case.

Reviewing the 15 murders, it was clear that the killer was currently operating in Terrebonne Parish, whose parish seat was Houma. As they got to work, the partially clad body of 23-year-old Kurt Cunningham was found floating in a ditch in Lafourche Parish. He was white and lived in Thibodaux. Last seen in Houma on 8 April, he was not found until 20 days later. The body was so badly decomposed that the cause of death could not be established.

Then, on 2 July 2005, the body of 28-year-old African American, Alonzo Hogan, was found in a cane field in St Charles Parish off Highway 306. He was fully clothed, but the autopsy ascertained that he had been sodomized and strangled. The body of 17-year-old African American and Houma resident, Wayne Smith, was found fully clothed in a ditch off Grand Caillou Road. The cause of death could not be determined.

The task force was hard at work on these cases when they were closed down by Hurricane Katrina, which hit on 28 August 2005. When the flood waters subsided, the body of an African American, Chris DeVille, was found fully clothed in a ditch off Highway 1 in Assumption Parish. He was 40. Unlike the other victims who had all been involved in crime in one way or another, DeVille came from a respectable family. His brother was even a cop. The body had been eaten by rats.

'When we found him, he was nothing. Nothing but bones,' said his sister Cynthia Barabin. 'We had to bury bones.'

Lucky break

Then the police got lucky. After serving time for a minor drug offence, John Banning was out on parole. By chance, his parole officer, Tom Lambert, was a member of the task force. Banning was out walking when Dominique pulled up beside him and asked if he wanted a beer. Then he pulled out the picture of an attractive white woman.

'How'd you like to f**k this white girl,' he asked. 'She'd really like to make it with a guy like you.'

This was Dominique's standard practice with straight guys. There were six or seven of them among his victims. Banning got in and Dominque drove him to Bayou Blue Road.

'Don't be surprised that I want to tie you up,' said Dominique.

Dominique pulled into his sister's yard and they went into his trailer there.

'I'll tie you up now,' Dominique told Banning. 'Take off your clothes.'

He would say that the woman he was to have sex with had been raped, hurt, so the man had to be tied up before they started. Normally, when Dominique got the man bound hand and foot, he would tell them that it was not true. There was no woman. At that point, he raped and murdered them.

Banning was suspicious. He looked around. The trailer was a mess, full of old clothes and stacks of gay porn. He made a dash for the door. Dominique did not attempt to stop him.

The net closes

Officer Lambert had already figured that some of his parolees had the same profile as the killer's victims, so he questioned them for clues. Banning told him of his encounter with a mysterious white guy who had wanted to tie him up. He led the police to Bayou Blue Road and the trailer that belonged to Ronald J Dominique.

Dominique agreed to accompany them to their headquarters where they told him of Banning's complaint. He said the bondage was just part of a sex game. Nevertheless, he was asked to provide DNA samples and consented. Then, they drove him back to his trailer. Back at headquarters, detectives pulled up his record. Among the charges that had been dropped were two counts of sodomy with men. But while they were building a case, there would be more victims.

Twenty-one-year-old Nick Pellegrin was working on his house when Dominique arrived to read the meter. Pellegrin, who was short of money, agreed to go out with Dominique, after he had finished work, to have some 'fun'. His body was found on 9 November 2005. He had been raped and strangled, and there were ligature marks around his wrists. The police had the killer within their grasp, yet he had killed again.

A few days later, the lab called, saying that they had a DNA match between Dominique and the chest hairs found on Oliver LeBanks' body. But it was a mitochondrial match. Mitochondrial DNA is inherited solely from the mother, so narrows the match only to members of the family and not to a specific individual. Dominique was put under surveillance 24-7.

There was another DNA match with semen left in Angel Mejia's rectum. Again, it was a mitochondrial match – not enough to convince a jury 'beyond reasonable doubt'.

Short of funds, local cops took to following Dominique on their own time. But on 15 October 2006, he managed to shake his tail. That day, 27-year-old Christopher Sutterfield disappeared after visiting friends in Houma. His body was dumped along Highway 69 in Iberville Parish near Baton Rouge. It was clear from the marks on his body that Dominique had killed again.

Frustrated, the police asked a judge for an arrest warrant on Ronald J Dominique for two first-degree murders – those of Oliver LeBanks and Manuel Reed. By this time, his sister was fed up with the surveillance and wanted no trouble with the police, so she kicked Dominique out. He moved to the Bunkhouse, a flophouse in Houma used by oil-rig workers, and was arrested there on 1 December 2006.

Dominique quickly confessed to the two murders – and to the murder of Michael Vincent. In all, he said he had killed 23 men and agreed to take the police to all the dump sites. In court, he pleaded guilty to eight murders where they had the best evidence rather than suffer the death penalty. He also admitted that he had raped all his victims before he strangled them, though those who did not consent to being tied up he let go.

On 23 September 2008, Ronald Dominique was sentenced to eight life sentences and was sent to the Louisiana State Penitentiary at Angola – the very last place he wanted to end up – where he will remain for the rest of his life.

CHAPTER 14

Alexander Yuryevich Pichushkin

1992–2006

Initially knows as The Bitsa Park Maniac after a wooded park in southeast Moscow where he committed his murders, Alexander Yuryevich Pichushkin became known as The Chessboard Killer after claiming that he intended to kill 64 people, one for each square of the chessboard.

He was convicted of 48 murders, after being charged with 49, and three attempted murders, but admitted to another 11. On a chessboard in his home, all except for one square had been crossed off. At first, he had aimed to outdo Russia's most notorious killer, The Rostov Ripper, Andrei Chikatilo, who was convicted of the murder and mutilation of 52 young women and children in 1992, confessing to 56.

Newspaper cuttings about Chikatilo were found in Pichushkin's flat, along with a large stash of pornography, much of it violent. Pichushkin easily surpassed Chikatilo's body count and, while approaching his stated target of 64, said he would have continued.

'If they [the police] had not caught me, I would never have stopped,' he said. 'For me, life without killing is like life without food for you.' Expressing no regrets, he said he felt a bond with his victims. 'I felt like the father of all these people, since it was I who opened the door for them to another world,' he said.

Opening gambit

He began killing as a student at the age of 18.

'The first was in 1992... it was my college mate.' Apparently, his school friend refused to join in the campaign of murder with him.

Pichushkin's father left the family when his son was only nine months old. Alexander was brought up by his mother and grandfather.

'I grew up together with Alexander,' said a neighbour's son. 'We had common friends and spent a lot of time together. Once when we were 15 years old, the boys beat him and after that he became withdrawn and aloof.'

Prematurely balding, Pichushkin was a shop assistant and an alcoholic who never had any friends or girlfriends.

'First of all, what is a friend?' asked Pichushkin. 'This is not someone who gives you one hundred roubles or lets you stay over for a night.'

Friends were someone you killed.

'I received more pleasure from killing people whom I knew personally,' he admitted. 'But I also found a way to get to strangers and that is not easy. Their relatives said that they would never go somewhere with a stranger. But to me they are flying, despite the difference in age, [such as] youngster, Koryagin [one of his victims]... I was leaving the police office and I knew that everywhere was an ambush, but I remained free. Then I spit and got caught.'

Otherwise, he was a quiet man who kept himself to himself.

'He would leave his flat every morning and come back only in the evening,' said the neighbour. 'He was as drunk as a fish and fell down near his door.'

He told police he killed for sport.

'It was all the same to me who I killed,' he said. 'I killed for the sake of the process itself. And, for the record, I wanted to kill as many people as possible and to beat Chikatilo's record.'

Pawns in his game

Pichushkin's campaign of murder got under way in earnest in the summer of 2001.

'It dawned upon me on that day that I would murder someone,' he said during his trial.

He began by befriending elderly homeless men, playing chess with them in the park. He would offer them vodka if they would join him in mourning his dead dog, which he had buried in a secluded area of the park. He said he had nightmares about that dog.

'It lived with me a long time,' he said. 'She died. It was my fault. I treated it, how you say, not very well. She could have been saved. It was a bad situation… it left something in my subconscious.'

He killed 11 people that year, including six in one month. Later, he also targeted younger men, women and children. Once they were drunk, he would hit them over the head with a hammer, an iron bar or a vodka bottle. He would always attack from behind to avoid spilling blood on his clothes. Unlike Chikatilo, he did not rape his victims, though he did sometimes stick his penis in the holes he had made in their skulls.

'I liked the sound of a skull splitting,' he told prosecutors.

He strangled a few of his victims and even tested out a home-made, single-shot gun made of pipe. He'd dump the bodies in a sewer, sometimes while they were still alive. Many victims were never found, though he took the police to the places where he had disposed of them.

Beginning in 2005, he began to kill with 'particular cruelty', hitting his intoxicated victims multiple times in the head with a hammer, then sticking an unfinished bottle of vodka into their shattered skulls, prosecutors said. He drew 'particular pleasure and satisfaction' from finishing off his victims as they 'pleaded for mercy'. By then, Pichushkin also no longer tried to conceal the bodies.

Wrong move

The police realized that a serial killer was at work. By February 2006, some 200 officers were deployed in the park after police received a tip-off that a man resembling the killer had been spotted. The officers detained a suspect, but he pulled out a knife and managed to break free from his handcuffs. He then tried to flee. Police shot the man in the leg, and he was hospitalized. But it was the wrong man.

Pichushkin was outraged. 'I was simply hurt, that my work was being attributed to someone else,' he said. He admitted that he killed one of his last victims in February 2006 to demonstrate that he was still at large following inaccurate reports in Russian newspapers that the Bitsa Maniac had been caught.

The police got their big break when the body of 36-year-old Marina Mosksalyova was found in a river in the Bitsa Park. She had suffered several blows to her head and small wooden stakes had been driven through her eyes and into her skull.

It turned out that she worked in the same shop as Pichushkin and had gone for a stroll in the park with him. She had left a note for her 15-year-old son beforehand, telling him that he was going with Pichushkin to visit his dog's grave. She had even written down his phone number and a metro ticket was found on her body. CCTV footage from Moscow's underground system showed her walking on the platform with him. Pichushkin said during the trial that he was aware of the note but 'I could not stop myself from killing her.'

Pichushkin was arrested on 16 June 2006 and began telling the police about all the other people he had killed. Initially, he was charged with the murder of two women on 11 and 16 April 2006, but prosecutors said that he was involved in another 46 homicides. At a bail hearing, he said that he was 'a punctual and law-abiding citizen, who will immediately turn up for questioning once the investigator summons him'. Bail was denied on the grounds that he might go into hiding, hamper the investigation or destroy evidence.

During his trial, Pichushkin was kept in a reinforced glass cage in the courtroom. He was unrepentant.

'I killed, so I could live myself: you kill someone and immediately feel relieved, your shoulders straighten up and you want to live,' he said.

During the trial his former employers describing him as 'disciplined and diligent' and 'polite and tactful'.

'Why are you studying me so thoroughly?' Pichushkin remarked from his cage.

His lawyer, Pavel Ivannikov, said that, despite his seemingly unrepentant and defiant behaviour during the trial, Pichushkin 'is afraid and wants to wiggle himself out'.

'He wants to convince us that what he was doing was right,' Ivannikov told the Associated Press. 'He imagined himself to be God. The one who decides who is to live and who is to die.'

Endgame

Pichushkin leant against the glass and stared down at the floor as the judge took about an hour to read the verdict. He was sentenced to life in prison, with the first 15 years in solitary confinement. The Russia Federation has maintained a moratorium on capital punishment as part of its obligations as a member of the Council of Europe which it only left in 2022, after 26 years, following the invasion of Ukraine.

Five months after his conviction, Pichushkin gave an interview to the Russian tabloid, *Tvoi Den*. He seemed to be adjusting well to incarceration.

'When I was brought to prison, I was not in a good mood,' he said. 'Now it's gotten better, I have completely adapted. They have ideal water here. It's so hot, I even have to dilute it with cold water. For all the time that I have been here, my hair was cut only once. Do you know how much time they give me to take a shower – five whole minutes!'

Still, he showed no remorse.

'No, I do not regret it,' he said. 'So much strength and time spent. Repent? I do not repent, this is again a dull formality. It will not change my sentence. Since I was young, I dreamed… Everything was different back then. And it all turned out the way I wanted it to. I knew that they had me nailed when they started pressing me about 12 victims, but then they were all surprised that I had actually killed 60.'

And he was enjoying his new-found fame.

'I watched a show about me on TV. Denis, my classmate, told the camera: "When we learned that he had committed these crimes it was a

Alexander Pichushkin, the Bitsa Park Maniac.

shock." Others said I was a rare case – killing just for the sake of killing. There is no motivation: neither race nor sex nor religion. Even someone wrote: "Pichushkin himself doesn't know yet that the history of criminology is changed, that it didn't account for someone such as him, that he will go down in history forever."'

Nor had his contempt for human life waned.

'Human life is not too long,' he said. 'It is cheaper than a sausage. My lawyer: I would cut him open like a fish. I would have killed him like an insect, and I would receive much pleasure from the process. I would cut him up and make belts out of his flesh. But as for remembering everyone I killed, who and when and where, that I don't remember. I don't even care to remember.'

Religion did not trouble him either.

'I was baptized when I was three-months old. The baptism took place, but I did not want it. Well, I do not think that someone… is there. I can also say that I will not either read the Bible or write an autobiography.'

Writing is for girls – and journalists, according to Pichushkin.

'I have never prayed to God, never will. This is a beautiful fairy tale for the weak, for those who sacrifice themselves to the state. Men, as they age, increasingly dream that someone is there who is all powerful. Well, what is it? As for voting, in all my 33 years I have never missed a chance to vote.'

Vladimir Putin was in power at the time.

His plans for the future?

'I would like to live in Mexico. First, it is warm there and, secondly, there are forests. Maybe I could live in a different way if I was there…'

When the *Tvoi Den* reporter told Puchushkin that Mexico doesn't have forests, he said: 'Do you want to tell me there are no jungles? Like Freddy Krueger said: "Elm Street exists in every city."'

CHAPTER 15

Tiffany Hall

September 2006

Twenty-four-year-old Tiffany Hall used to babysit for her old schoolfriend, 23-year-old mother-of-three, Jimella Tunstall, at her apartment in the John DeShields Housing Project in East St Louis. Then, on 15 September 2004, when Jimella was seven months pregnant, Hall hit her best friend over the head with a chair leg and bound her arms and legs with duct tape.

When Jimella tried to wriggle free, Hall hit her again and taped her mouth shut. Then, she dragged the unconscious woman into the bathroom. In the bathtub, Hall cut the foetus from Jimella's stomach using a pair of scissors and left her to bleed to death.

Illinois State police investigator, David Bivens, told the coroner's jury that Hall 'had been thinking about taking the baby for some time'.

Jimella's body was first hidden in a plastic container in the basement, then dragged outside and hidden in tall weeds behind the block.

A few hours later, Hall summoned the police to Frank Holten Park – just blocks from where Jimella's body was later found – where she claimed she had given birth to a stillborn child. The premature birth, she said, had been brought on alternately by consensual sex or rape. Taken to hospital, the dead baby showed no signs of trauma and a postmortem the following day failed to determine a cause of death. Hall herself refused to be examined.

Three days later, Hall visited the father of two of Tunstall's children as well as the unborn child. He was looking after all three of Jimella's children – DeMond Tunstall, seven, Ivan Tunstall-Collins, two, and Jinella Tunstall, one. Hall told him that Jimella wanted her to pick up the children and that was the last he saw of them. Hall took them back to Jimella's apartment where she drowned them in the bath where their mother had died.

On 21 September, while the police were out searching for the missing children, Hall attended the funeral of the stolen foetus with her boyfriend, reportedly a sailor on shore leave. She told him that the baby was not his and that she had killed the mother to get it. He called the police and she was arrested.

Charged with first-degree murder and the intentional homicide of an unborn child, Hall was held on a $5-million bond. Initially, she pleaded not guilty, but then she admitted drowning the three children and told the authorities where to find their bodies. They were in a washer and a dryer in Jimella's apartment that had been overlooked in the search.

Hall faced the death penalty, but pleaded guilty in court and was sentenced to life imprisonment without the possibility of parole.

CHAPTER 16

Sulejman Talović

12 February 2007

At 6.44pm on 12 February 2007, 18-year-old Sulejman Talović, a Bosniak refugee from Bosnia and Herzegovina, went to the Trolley Square Mall in Salt Lake City, Utah, his regular hang-out. But that evening, he was carrying a shotgun, a .38-calibre handgun and a backpack full of ammunition. He shot and killed five people, including a girl of 15, and injured another four.

Marie Smith, the 23-year-old store manager at Bath & Body, said she had seen the gunman through the store window. She watched as he raised his gun and fired at a young woman approaching him from behind.

'His expression stayed totally calm. He didn't seem upset, or like he was on a rampage,' said Smith, who crawled to an employee restroom to hide with others. He looked like 'an average Joe,' she said.

One of the wounded shoppers, 34-year-old Shawn Munns, was alone outside the mall after having a meal with his wife and two stepchildren when Talović blasted him with a shotgun. With dozens of pellets in his side, Munns staggered into a restaurant and warned diners about the gunman.

Barrage of gunfire

Forty-four-year-old Matt Lund was visiting his wife, Barbara, manager of the Secret Garden children's clothing store, when he heard the first shots. The couple and three others hid in a storage room for about 40 minutes, but were able to hear what was going on outside.

'We heard them say: "Police! Drop your weapon!" Then we heard shotgun fire. Then there was a barrage of gunfire,' said Lund. 'It was hard to believe.'

Off-duty policeman Kenneth Hammond was in the mall with his pregnant wife, Sarita, a 911 dispatcher. While Kenneth traded shots with Talović, Sarita borrowed a cell phone from a waiter and put in a 911 call. A SWAT team arrived and a marksman shot and killed Talović.

Thirty-three-year-old Hammond had been at the mall for an early Valentine's Day dinner with his wife. He said he first thought the sound of gunfire was construction noise but drew his gun and told his wife to call the police when he realized what was happening.

'I've been in situations before where I've had to chase a guy who was pointing a gun at me,' he said.

Hammond was credited with drawing the gunman's attention until other officers could reach the scene. Talović was killed, although it was unclear who fired the fatal shot.

'I feel like I was there and did what I had to do,' Hammond said. He didn't feel like a hero, he added.

'We were there for a reason. I had my gun on me for a reason. We decided to eat dessert, which we never do, for a reason. Everything happened for a reason.'

Twenty-nine-year-old antiques store owner Barrett Dodds said he had seen a man in a trench coat exchanging gunfire with a police officer outside a card store. The gunman, he said, was backed into a children's clothing store.

'I saw the shooter go down,' said Dodds, who watched from the second floor.

Visiting from Washington, DC, 60-year-old Barb McKeown was in another antiques shop when two frantic women ran in saying they had heard gunshots.

'Then we heard shot after shot after shot – loud, loud, loud,' said McKeown. She thought she heard about 20. She and three other people hid under a staircase until it was safe to leave.

On the way out, Lund said he saw a woman's body face-down at the entrance to the Pottery Barn Kids store and a man's body on the floor in the mall's east-west corridor.

'There were a lot of blown-out store windows and shotgun shell casings all over the floor,' Lund said. 'It was quite surreal.'

Victim of war

There is some suggestion that Talović suffered from a mental condition, having lived in Sarajevo during the Bosnian War. He is also alleged to have shouted: 'Allahu Akbar!' during the shooting. However, the police did not suspect terrorism.

He was buried in his birthplace, the small village of Talovići near Cerska, Bosnia and Herzegovina, which was in the Srebrenica enclave overrun by the Serbs in the Bosnian War. His family had emigrated to the US in 1998. He had received his green card in 2005 and lived with his mother in Salt Lake City. He had a record of petty juvenile crime and had dropped out of high school at the age of 16, though he often attended Friday prayers at the Al-Noor mosque in Salt Lake City.

Talović's aunt, Ajka Omerović, who also lived in Utah, said relatives had no idea why the young man attacked so many strangers. She said that, as a child, Talović had lived in Sarajevo, which had been under siege during the war.

'He was such a good boy. I don't know what happened,' she told Salt Lake City television station KSL-TV.

However, his father blamed the American government.

'In the US, you cannot buy cigarettes if you are under age, but you can buy a gun,' he said.

CHAPTER 17

Seung-hui Cho

16 April 2007

It became known as the Virginia Tech Massacre when 23-year-old senior-level undergraduate, Seung-hui Cho, killed 32 fellow students and faculty members, and wounded seven more. He had undergone court-ordered psychiatric treatment. His family found him uncommunicative – indeed, mute – his roommates thought him weird. Female students complained of harassment. He had been excluded from classes for menacing behaviour. His written work was disturbing and violent. Yet, he was still able to purchase firearms under Virginia law.

So, at around 6.45am on 16 April 2007, he entered West Ambler Johnston Hall, a co-ed residence at the college that housed 894 students, carrying two handguns – a 9mm Glock 19 and a .22-calibre Walther P22.

On the fourth floor, he went to the room of 19-year-old freshman Emily Hilscher. She had just returned home after a night out with her boyfriend. Not long after 7.15am, shots were heard. The police could find no motive for her slaying. They found no evidence that Cho knew Hilscher or any of the other students killed in the rampage.

Resident assistant, Ryan Clark, a 22-year-old senior, heard the shots and went to investigate. He, too, was shot and killed. Cho fled the scene, leaving bloody footprints, and went back to his dorm room in Harper Hall, two-minutes' walk away.

While the emergency medical services units rushed to the scene of the killing, Cho changed out of his bloodstained clothes and logged on to his computer to delete his emails and wipe out his account. He then removed the hard drive and disposed of it, along with his mobile phone, probably throwing them in the campus duck pond, though they have never been found.

It appears that he also planned to dispose of the guns as the serial numbers had been filed off.

Less than two hours after the murder of Hilscher and Clark, Cho was seen at a post office off campus where he mailed a package to NBC News in New York. Inside the package were pictures of Cho brandishing his guns, two rambling letters and videos Cho had shot of himself. In them, he railed against society and how it had ill-treated him. He also mentioned the 1999 Columbine High School killers, Eric Harris and Dylan Klebold, by name, indicating that he too craved fame through mass killing.

'I didn't have to do this. I could have left. I could have fled. But no, I will no longer run. It's not for me. For my children, for my brothers and sisters that you fucked, I did it for them,' he wrote. 'When the time came, I did it. I had to.'

He also compared himself to Jesus Christ and said that his death would 'inspire generations of weak and defenceless people'.

Escalating violence

After posting the package, Cho headed for Norris Hall, which housed the Engineering, Science and Mechanics faculties. He was carrying a backpack that contained the two handguns, 19 ten- and 15-round rapid-loading magazines – almost 400 rounds of ammunition – and heavy chains that he used to chain the three main entrance doors shut. He placed a note on one of the doors, warning that a bomb would go off if anyone tried to remove the chains.

At around 9.30am, Cho walked into room 206, where Professor G. V. Loganathan was teaching a class on advanced hydrology. He shot and killed the professor. Without a word, he turned his gun on the students, killing nine of the 13 students in the room and injuring two others. Only two survived unharmed. Hearing the shots, Jocelyne Couture-Nowak, who was teaching French in room 211, asked student Colin Goddard to call the police on his cell phone.

Next, Cho moved across the hall to room 207, where Christopher Bishop was teaching German. Cho shot Bishop and several students near the doorway, then moved down the aisle of the classroom, shooting others. Bishop and four others died; six were wounded.

In room 211, the students tried to barricade the door, but Cho pushed his way in. He shot Jocelyne Couture-Nowak, killing her, and moved down the aisle, firing at the students. Again, Cho said nothing. Colin Goddard was among the first to be shot, though he survived. But another student, Emily Haas, picked up his mobile phone and stayed on the line while the shooting went on. Even though she was wounded twice in the head, she spoke quietly to the dispatcher, then closed her eyes and played dead.

Hearing gunshots, students in room 205 lay on the floor, while student Zach Petkewicz barricaded the door with a large table. Unable to force his way in, Cho fired through the door several times, but no one was hit.

Cho returned to room 207, but four survivors held the door closed. Nevertheless, he managed to force the door open an inch and fired about five shots around the door, before giving up. Returning to room 211, he walked up and down the aisles, shooting students at point-blank range. There were few places for the students to hide, except behind their desks, which afforded little cover. Colin Goddard, who was playing dead, was shot twice more, though he survived. But the teacher and 11 students lay dead. Another six were wounded. Everyone in the entire class had fallen victim to Cho's bullets.

After reloading, Cho then tried to enter room 204 where Professor Liviu Librescu, a 76-year-old Holocaust survivor, was teaching mechanics. He braced his body against the door, while students leapt through the windows. A shot through the door killed Librescu. Two students were shot as they were making their escape through the window. In all, four students in the mechanics class were shot, one fatally.

The massacre in Norris Hall continued for about ten to 12 minutes. In that time, Cho had murdered 25 students and five faculty members. Another 15 were shot and survived, though the hollow-tipped bullets Cho had used

Seung-hui Cho, perpetrator of the Virginia Tech Massacre.

caused terrible injuries. Six more were injured when they jumped from the windows. Cho ended the carnage by returning to room 211 and shooting himself in the head as the police closed in.

Mental health issues

The question was: could anyone have predicted that Cho would become a mass murderer? As a child in South Korea, he was plagued with health problems. He was extremely quiet and sweet-natured but had few friends. When he was eight, his parents moved to the US in the hope of improving their children's educational opportunities. Cho and his older sister spoke no English and became isolated. Within two years, they had learned English, but Cho could not read and write Korean, which the family used at home.

Cho spoke little at home and, at school, he would not interact with other children. His family feared he might be autistic, but there was no official diagnosis. He went into therapy. But by eighth grade, his therapist feared that he might be suicidal.

In 1999, during the spring of Cho's eighth grade year, the Columbine High School massacre made national news. Cho was transfixed by it.

'I remember sitting in Spanish class with him, right next to him, and there being something written on his binder to the effect of, you know, "F" you all, I hope you all burn in hell," which I would assume meant us, the students,' said a classmate. Cho also wrote in a school assignment about wanting to 'repeat Columbine'.

The school contacted Cho's sister, who reported the incident to their parents. Cho was sent to a psychiatrist. However, he was gifted in science and mathematics, and it was clear that he should go to college. A counsellor urged that he be sent to a small college close to home, but Cho was determined to go to Virginia Tech. Once there, he remained withdrawn.

Cho had ambitions to write a novel, but his ideas were rejected by New York publishing houses. He then got into heavy metal. To the annoyance of his roommates, he listened repeatedly to Collective Soul's 'Shine' and wrote the lyrics 'Teach me how to speak; Teach me how to share; Teach me where to go' on his dormitory room wall.

In poetry classes, he would appear wearing reflective sunglasses and a hat pulled down over his face. When he read, his voice was inaudible. What he wrote was dark, obscene and violent, and he accused his classmates who ate meat of being complicit in the massacre of animals.

'If you despicable human beings who are all disgraces to the human race keep this up, before you know it you will turn into cannibals – eating little babies, your friends,' he wrote. 'I hope y'all burn in hell for mass murdering and eating all those little animals.'

He photographed girls' legs under the desks and students grew afraid of him. His teacher had him removed from her class, saying she would resign rather than continue teaching him. His written work continued in its dark vein. In one story, the protagonist, clearly based on himself, tells a 'gothic girl': 'I'm nothing. I'm a loser. I can't do anything. I was going to kill every god damn person in this damn school, swear to god I was, but I... couldn't. I just couldn't. Damn it, I hate myself!' That autumn, he took a class called 'Contemporary Horror'.

He started stalking female students. The police warned him to stop. Instead, he turned to text messaging, emails and Facebook. One recipient grew fearful and called the police. Cho was found to be mentally ill, but, as he did not seem to be a danger to himself or others, he was not hospitalized, though he was ordered to present himself for a psychiatric assessment and given treatment as an outpatient.

On the night before the massacre, Cho made his regular Sunday call to his parents. They suspected nothing.

Flags at half-mast

After the massacre, police found a suicide note in Cho's dorm room that included deprecatory comments about 'rich kids', 'debauchery' and 'deceitful charlatans'. In the material he sent to NBC, he said: 'You forced me into a corner and gave me only one option... You just loved to crucify me. You loved inducing cancer in my head, terror in my heart and ripping my soul all this time.'

While Cho included threatening messages to the then US president, George W Bush, Vice President, Dick Cheney, and Secretary of State, Condoleezza Rice, after the massacre, flags on the White House were flown at half-mast, but this had little effect on the gun-control debate. Indeed, proponents of gun rights and the Second Amendment argued that Virginia Tech's gun-free 'safe zone' policy ensured that none of the students or faculty would be armed, guaranteeing that no one could stop Cho's rampage.

The Economist concluded: 'The Columbine killings of 1999 failed to provoke any shift in Americans' attitudes to guns. There is no reason to believe that this massacre, or the next one, will do so either.'

Flags at half-mast at Virginia Tech.

CHAPTER 18

Pekka-Eric Auvinen

7 November 2007

The Columbine High School massacre of 1999 resulted in the deaths of 15, including the two perpetrators, with 24 wounded. It provoked copy-cat killings around the world, even as far away as Finland. Like Harris and Klebold, the perpetrator, 18-year-old student Pekka-Eric Auvinen, sought to explain his motives by shooting videos and posting them online.

At about 11.40am on 7 November, he walked into Jokela High School in Tuusula, southern Finland, and opened fire, slaughtering his fellow students in the entrance way. The headmistress, 61-year-old Helena Kalmi, called the police, then ordered pupils and teachers to barricade themselves in their classrooms.

Instead of seeking safety herself, Kalmi went out to confront the gunman. Auvinen forced her to her knees in the school yard, then shot her seven times in full view of pupils watching from a classroom window. The 43-year-old school nurse who went to the aid of injured students was shot and killed, too. And a 25-year-old single mother, taking an adult training class at the school, was also found dead.

Auvinen then began walking around the school, firing through classroom doors and shooting people at random. The victims sustained multiple injuries to head and upper body. Some had been shot up to 20 times. Soon, five boys between 16 and 18 lay dead. But he also pointed his gun at some people without shooting them.

Shouting orders at students, he proclaimed that he was starting a revolution. He seems to have planned the attack to coincide with the anniversary of the Bolshevik revolution in Russia in 1917. Until then, Finland had been part of the Russian Empire and gained short-lived independence.

He urged the students to destroy school property. Dousing the walls and floor of the main corridor with two-stroke fuel, he tried to set it alight, but the mixture of petrol and oil failed to ignite.

The police arrived at 11.55, but when they tried to start negotiations, they were met with a hail of bullets. Soon the school was surrounded by 100 officers, including a special operations unit. Even off-duty police officers turned up. In just 20 minutes, Auvinen had loosed off 69 rounds.

The attack ended at 12.24, when Auvinen turned the gun on himself, even though he still had over 320 live bullets left and was carrying a 22-calibre Sig Sauer Mosquito pistol capable of firing ten rounds in five seconds.

Acting ultra-cautiously, the police held off storming the school until 1.53pm, more than two hours after they had first been called. Auvinen was found in a school toilet, unconscious but still alive. He was taken to Helsinki University Central Hospital but died from his injuries that evening.

Obsessed with guns

During their investigation, the police discovered that Auvinen had been a victim of school bullying for years. Born locally, he was part of a conventional two-parent family. His father was a musician; his mother was a deputy on Tuusula municipal council. He also had an 11-year-old brother.

One of his teachers said Auvinen was above average academically and took an interest in history, philosophy and politics – particularly extreme right- and left-wing movements. On his YouTube user page, he described himself as 'a cynical existentialist, antihuman humanist, antisocial social Darwinist, realistic idealist and godlike atheist'. He had been on anti-depressants since he was 17. These sometimes induce suicidal tendencies as a side-effect in adolescents.

The massacre had not been long in the planning. Auvinen had only received his gun licence three weeks before the school shootings. He was a registered member of the Helsinki Shooting Club but had only attended a single one-hour training session.

His weapon, a SIG Sauer Mosquito .22-calibre handgun, had been obtained legally and was registered to Auvinen on 19 October. Auvinen himself wanted to buy a more powerful Beretta 9mm pistol, but his application was rejected by police. In Finland, the police usually require a hobby shooter to begin with a .22-calibre weapon. In the weeks before the shootings, he had uploaded a video of himself shooting his new gun. It was called 'Me and My Gun, Catherine. I Love Her.'

Pekka-Eric Auvinen holding his gun in a homemade video he uploaded to YouTube.

An hour before the shooting, Auvinen uploaded another video called the 'Jokela High School Massacre – 11/7/2007' to YouTube. KMFDM's song, 'Stray Bullet', was used as a soundtrack. This track was also used by Columbine shooter Eric Harris on his website. Auvinen's username was 'Sturmgeist89'. *Sturmgeist* means 'Storm Spirit' in German.

Many of his other YouTube videos were about other shootings and violent incidents, including the Columbine High School massacre, the Waco siege in Texas in 1993 where federal agents besieged the compound of the Branch Davidian sect, killing 86, the Tokyo sarin gas attack where the Aum Shinrikyo sect poisoned 13 people on the underground in 1995 and the 'shock and awe' bombing during the invasion of Iraq in 2003.

He also uploaded a selection of scenes from *Schindler's List*, in which Jews are tortured and killed, a tribute to Columbine killers Eric Harris and Dylan Klebold and a post glorifying the last days of the Twin Towers. American serial killer and cannibal Jeffrey Dahmer, and a tribute to Theodore Kaczynski, the US anti-government terrorist known as the Unabomber, also featured in his macabre posts.

A spokesman for the cybercrime department of Helsinki police said: 'It's highly probable that there was some form of contact between Pekka-Eric Auvinen and Dillon Cosey', a 14-year-old boy arrested the month before on suspicion of planning an attack on his school in a suburb of Philadelphia. Acting on a tip-off, the police found a 9mm semi-automatic rifle, handmade grenades, a .22 pistol and a .22 single-shot rifle at Cosey's home.

Less than two weeks later, Auvinen, already a member of a shooting club, was buying his first gun – a .22 pistol – and expressing interest in a 9mm semi-automatic. The police do not believe this to have been a coincidence. The two youths are thought to have made contact over two MySpace groups, 'RIP Eric and Dylan' – a reference to Eric Harris and Dylan Klebold – and 'Natural Selection'.

So that people would get to know him a little better, Auvinen posted a personal profile on the web. It read:

Occupation: Unemployed Philosopher, Outcast
Companies: Human Race (evolved one step above though)
Interests and Hobbies: Existentialism, Freedom, Truth, Misanthropy, Social/Personality Psychology, Evolution Science, Political Incorrectness, Women, BDSM, Guns (I love you Catherine), Shooting, Computer Games, Sarcasm, Irony, Mass/Serial Killers, Macabre Art, Black Comedy, Absurdism
Movies and Shows: The Matrix, A View To A Kill, Falling Down, Natural Born Killers, Reservoir Dogs, Last Man Standing, Full Metal Jacket, Dr Butcher MD (aka Zombie Holocaust), Saw 1–3, Lord Of War, The Deer Hunter, True Romance, The Untouchables, 28 Days Later, 28 Weeks Later, Idiocracy, They Live, Apocalypse Now, End Of Days, The Shining, The Dead Zone, Dr Strangelove, House MD (TV), Monty Python (TV) Documentaries Relating To History
Music: KMFDM, Rammstein, Eisbrecher, Nine Inch Nails, Grendel, Impaled Nazarene, Macabre, Deathstars, The Prodigy, Combichrist, Godsmack, Slayer, Children of Bodom, Alice Cooper, Sturmgeist, Suicide Commando, Hatebreed, Suffocation, Terrorizer
Books: Fahrenheit 451 (Bradbury), 1984 (Orwell), Brave New World (Huxley), The Republic (Plato), all works of Nietzsche

Twisted mind

Auvinen also posted a manifesto on the internet, which aimed to explain his actions. Part of it read:

I am prepared to fight and die for my cause. I, as a natural selector, will eliminate all who I see unfit, disgraces of human race and failures of natural selection.

You might ask yourselves, why did I do this and what do I want. Well, most of you are too arrogant and closed-minded to understand... You will probably say me that I am 'insane', 'crazy', 'psychopath', 'criminal' or crap like that. No, the truth is that I am just an animal, a human, an individual, a dissident.

I have had enough. I don't want to be part of this fucked up society. Like some other wise people have said in the past, human race is not worth fighting for or saving... only worth killing. But when my enemies will run and hide in fear when mentioning my name... when the gangsters of the corrupted governments have been shot in the streets... when the rule of idiocracy and the democratic system has been replaced with justice... when intelligent people are finally free and rule the society instead of the idiocratic rule of majority... in that great day of deliverance, you will know what I want.

Long live the revolution... revolution against the system, which enslaves not only the majority of weak-minded masses but also the small minority of strong-minded and intelligent individuals! If we want to live in a different world, we must act. We must rise against the enslaving, corrupted and totalitarian regimes and overthrow the tyrants, gangsters and the rule of idiocracy. I can't alone change much but hopefully my actions will inspire all the intelligent people of the world and start some sort of revolution against the current systems. The system discriminating again nature and justice is my enemy. The people living in the world of delusion and supporting this system are my enemies.

I am ready to die for a cause I know is right, just and true... even if I would lose or the battle would be only remembered as evil... I will rather fight and die than live a long and unhappy life.

And remember that this is my war, my ideas and my plans. Don't blame anyone else for my actions than myself. Don't blame my parents or my friends. I told nobody about my plans and I always kept them inside my mind only. Don't blame the movies I see, the music I hear, the games I play or the books I read. No, they had nothing to do with this. This is my war: one man war against humanity, governments and weak-minded masses of the world! No mercy for the scum of the earth! HUMANITY IS OVERRATED! It's time to put NATURAL SELECTION & SURVIVAL OF THE FITTEST back on tracks!

Justice renders to everyone his due.

CHAPTER 19

Robert A. Hawkins

5 December 2007

Nineteen-year-old Robert A. Hawkins had been plagued with mental health problems throughout his short life. At the age of six, he was hospitalized for depression. At 14, he was undergoing psychiatric treatment after threatening to kill his stepmother with an axe. He then became a ward of the State of Nebraska and was hospitalized again with various disorders, including attention deficit disorder, an unspecified mood disorder, oppositional defiant disorder and parent-child relationship problems. His treatment cost the state $265,000.

He dropped out of school. Estranged from his parents, he went to live with two friends and their mother, Debora Maruca-Kovac, who described him as 'troubled'. He became depressed when he lost his job at McDonald's after being accused of stealing $17. Then he split up with his girlfriend.

He accused a local teenager of stealing his CD player and threatened to kill her. With one felony drug conviction already on his record, he was arrested for delinquency and under-aged possession of alcohol on 24 November 2007. He was due to appear in court on 7 December, but a suicide note was found by his landlady on 5 December. It read:

Family
I'm so sorry for what I've put you through I never meant to hurt all of you so much and I don't blame any one of you for disowning me I just can't be a burden to you and my friends any longer You are all better off without me. I'm so sorry for this.

I've just snapped I can't take this meaningless existence anymore I've been a constant disappointment and that trend would have only continued. Just remember the good times we had together.

I love you mommy
I love you dad
I love you Kira
I love you Valancia
I love you Cynthia
I love you Zach
I love you Cayla
I love you Mark (P.S. I'm really sorry)

——

Friends
To all of my friends I'm so sorry for what I've done to you and put you through. I've been a peice of shit my entire life it seems this is my only option. I know everyone will remember me as some sort of monster but please understand that I just don't want to be a burden on the ones that I care for my entire life. I just want to take a few peices of shit with me. I love all of you so much and I don't want anyone to miss me just think about how much better you are off without me to support. I want my friends to remember all the good times we had together. Just think tho I'm gonna be fuckin famous. You guys have always been there for me I'm just sad that I'm gonna have to go this alone. You guys are the best friends anyone could ever ask for. That's all I have to say is that I fuckin love you guys.

P.S. I didn't eat that fuckin sandwich or the toielet thing either!

——

My will
I'm giving my car back to my mom and my friends can have whatever else I leave behind.

He signed the note and attached his social security number.

All hell breaks loose

An hour after the suicide note was delivered to the police at around 1.36pm, Hawkins walked into the Von Maur department store in the Westroads Mall in Omaha, Nebraska. He had a military-style haircut and wore a camouflage vest with a black backpack .

After walking a short distance into the store, he paused for a second, then turned around and left. Returning six minutes later through the same entrance, he proceeded directly to the elevator on his immediate right, this time carrying a commercial copy of the AKM 7.62x39mm semi-automatic rifle stolen from his stepfather's house, along with two 30-round magazines, concealed in a sweatshirt. He took the elevator to the top floor.

At about 1.43pm, Hawkins stepped out of the elevator on the third floor and opened fire. He killed eight people and wounded four others over the course of six minutes, before dying from a self-inflicted gunshot wound to the head near the customer service desk. He fired more than 30 rounds, hitting 12 people. Six died on the spot; one died before reaching the hospital, and another died 45 minutes after reaching the Emergency Room. Two others were critically injured but survived.

Omaha Police arrived at Westroads Mall about six minutes after the first 911 call. During the entire 70 seconds of that first call, all the dispatcher heard was gunshots.

Witness Jennifer Kramer told CNN she heard at least 25 shots.

'He just kept firing,' she said. She called 911 on her cell phone, whispering into it out of fear of being heard. A dispatcher told her other calls had been received and help was on the way, but she said it seemed to take 'a long time' for them to arrive.

'It was just so loud, and then it was silence,' she said. 'I was scared to death he'd be walking around looking for someone else.'

She said that, as she was being escorted out by police, she saw a man lying injured by the escalator where she had been previously.

'All of us were slightly confused because we didn't know what it was,' said mall employee, Charissa Tatoon, after hearing the first burst of gunfire.

'Immediately after that, there was a series of maybe 20 to 25 more shots up on the third floor,' she said. 'I was in the women's shoe department and there was a gentleman coming down the escalator that was very near the shoe department, and he was heard saying that he was calling 911, and immediately after that, the shooter shot down from the third floor and shot him on the second floor.'

'I saw employees taking a bunch of people into the dressing room, but I didn't want to go,' shopper Jennifer Kramer said. 'I didn't know if this guy was going to come looking for people in dressing rooms, so we hid in a pants rack towards the back of the men's department.'

A police car outside the Westroads Mall in Omaha, Nebraska.

Shocking scenes

Mickey Vickory, who worked in the store's third-floor service department, said she heard shots and went with co-workers and customers into a back closet, emerging about half an hour later when police told them to come out with their hands up. As police led them to another part of the mall for safety, they saw the victims.

'We saw the bodies and we saw the blood,' she said.

Keith Fidler, another Von Maur employee, said he heard a burst of five to six shots followed by 15 to 20 more rounds. Fidler said he huddled in the corner of the men's clothing department with about a dozen other employees until police yelled to get out of the store.

Witness Shawn Vidlak said the shots sounded like a nail gun. At first, he thought it was noise from construction work at the mall.

'People started screaming about gunshots,' Vidlak said. 'I grabbed my wife and kids. We got out of there as fast as we could.'

Witnesses described chaos as frantic shoppers fled from the store. Some shoppers and mall employees hid in clothes racks, dressing rooms and bathrooms.

'You're in such shock, it's hard to think. I was hoping God would spare us,' said a woman, clutching a rosary in her trembling hand after the shootings. 'We had to put up our hands and follow the police to the outside.'

Kirsty Wright and a friend were about to enter the store when she heard the shooting.

'We were steps away from walking in there,' she said. 'I can't imagine what it must have been like for the people who were in there.'

Fortunately, they stopped short because her friend wanted to use the restroom.

'Two minutes passed, or we would have been in there,' Wright said.

Hawkins shot some of his victims in the children's department.

'I always go straight to that department,' Wright said, 'because I have a nine-year-old.'

They were inside the mall, just outside the Von Maur store, when she heard gunshots.

'I heard what seemed like the first four or five, then there was a bigger round,' she said. 'What we didn't realize, what we found out later that night, was that we had heard someone being shot.'

When she realized what was happening, she yelled: 'There's a shooter.'

She tried to turn and run, but her legs wouldn't move fast enough. She said her friend was frozen in fear and they took refuge in a nearby jewellery store. The manager took them and four employees to a room at the back of the store. Wright said she sat in the small room wondering if a shooter would walk in the door any minute.

'Now I know what it felt like at Virginia Tech,' she said. 'Just waiting for your turn. Waiting for the door to fly open and for him to come in there, and it's your turn.'

Pallbearers carry a casket of one of the victims from the Westroads Mall shooting.

Kirsty Wright did not sleep well that night and the following day sought counselling. And there were unanswered questions.

'There was a woman in front of me in the checkout line at another store in the mall. She turned to her companion and said, "Let's go to Von Maur now,"' Wright said. 'I wonder what happened to her,' Wright said.

Little, lost puppy

A postmortem of Hawkins showed that he had 200 nanograms per millilitre of Valium in his system, which is towards the low end of its therapeutic-use range, which stretches from 100-1500 ng/mL. No trace of any other drug was found in his system.

Mrs Maruca-Kovac said that Hawkins 'reminded me of a lost puppy that nobody wanted' after being kicked out by his family. He had come to live with her about a year and a half before, telling her he could not stay with his own family because of 'some issues with his stepmother and him'.

'He came to us like a little lost puppy,' she said. 'He was always very sensitive and caring, always wanting to know how everybody was doing. He just needed a chance to get on his feet. We never saw violence in him.'

She said she was unaware Hawkins had any guns, although she said he knew a lot about them, as did his stepfather. However, the night before the shooting he had shown her and her two sons a Russian army rifle of the same type that was used. She thought it belonged to one of his relatives. She said she didn't think much of it – the gun looked too old to work.

'When he first came to live with us, he was in the foetal position and chewed his fingernails all the time,' she said. 'He had a lot of emotional problems, obviously.'

But she said she thought he was improving. Although he had dropped out of school and tried and failed to get into the Army, he had got a job, a haircut and a girlfriend. However, she said Hawkins and his girlfriend had broken up in the last couple of weeks, and he had taken it hard.

Mrs Maruca-Kovac said that Hawkins had left home at about 11am and called the house two hours later, sounding upset.

'He just said he wanted to thank me for everything I'd done for him… and he was sorry,' Mrs Maruca-Kovac said.

'I said: "Come home and we'll talk about it,"' she said. 'He said: "It's too late." He said he'd left a note, explaining everything.

'I was fearful that he was going to try to commit suicide. But I had no idea that he would involve so many other families. I feel so sorry for him, that he was so lost and alone that he had to resort to this.'

CHAPTER 20

Steven Kazmierczak

14 February 2008

Shortly before 3pm on 14 February 2008, a figure dressed in black, wearing a black knitted cap and a sweatshirt, burst into an oceanography class in the Cole Hall at Northern Illinois University in DeKalb. The topic of the day was the properties of the ocean floor and the instructor, Joseph Peterson, was doing his best to keep his hundred-plus students engaged. He was standing on stage at the front of the 300-seat auditorium, clicking through a PowerPoint presentation.

Standing just a few metres from the side door, the intruder produced a shotgun from a guitar case.

'He stood there for a second, looked and then just started shooting,' said Meghan Murphy, a 22-year-old junior from Western Springs. 'His face was blank, like he wasn't a person. He was a statue, aiming.'

Bullets fly

Instructor Peterson ducked and was shot in the arm.

'Nothing seemed out of place,' said junior, Doug Quesnel, 22. 'It was weird. He walked through there, but nothing seemed wrong until the shots went off.'

'It was just surreal,' said Dan Sweeney, also 22. 'Even when the first shot was fired, I couldn't believe it was happening. It didn't seem to register with anyone.'

'He just fires right into the audience,' said John Giovanni, 20. 'He didn't say a word. It didn't look like he was aiming directly at someone. I think he was trying to hit as many people as he could.'

'It didn't even sound like I thought a gun would sound like,' said Desiree Smith, a senior from Bolingbrook studying journalism. 'It sounded like a cork coming out of a champagne bottle.'

The gunfire threw the room into screaming chaos, with students crawling and running, shoving their way to the doors behind the rear seats.

'I dropped to the ground under my seat and could see another girl down there,' said Desiree Smith. 'We just stared at each other. I grabbed her leg and was squeezing it for about five seconds. Then, we moved all of a sudden. Everyone was army-crawling toward the back of the auditorium on the floor.

'As soon as I reached the door, I got halfway hunched over, and then started to run as soon as I got outside. I just ran. Everything went quiet around me and I felt I wasn't running fast enough. I remember thinking: "He's gonna shoot me, he's gonna shoot me."'

Half the class bolted for the doors; the rest cowered on the floor and attempted to hide under their seats or under desks, said 18-year-old Loren Weese, who was seated on the aisle about halfway up the auditorium.

'A lot of people fell,' she said. 'I don't know if they did that on purpose to avoid being shot. I remember stepping over them. I didn't talk to anybody.'

Daniel Parmenter, a 20-year-old sophomore finance major who worked on the university newspaper, the *Northern Star*, was sitting in the first row with his girlfriend when he was shot in the head. She was injured.

'I was prepared for one of the bullets to hit me in the back,' said junior, Shane Pope, 21, who was sitting towards the back. 'I was prepared for that to be my last moment.'

Harold Ng, also 21, a junior in communications, said the danger didn't register even after the firing started.

'I was still in the dream state and I didn't think it was reality. It was like a video game,' he said.

It wasn't until the other students in the class began to flee in panic that he, too, began to run, leaving his book bag and jacket on the floor of the auditorium. As he fled, he was shot in the back of the head.

'I didn't feel any pain or anything,' he said. 'I just swiped the back of my head with my hand, and then when I looked at my hand it was all bloody.'

He ran into neighbouring Neptune Hall, where other students noticed his wounds and helped him.

'The ambulance came in a short time and they were fast about it,' he said. 'I have three pellets in my head, but they said I'd be OK.'

John Giovanni, 20, of Des Plaines left his notebook and iPod behind as he crouched low and bolted for the door, figuring that a moving target would be harder to hit.

'I was pushing through people,' he said. 'You need to get out. You never know how good of a marksman he is... My goal was getting out of there and running as far as I could to be safe.'

When the gunman had exhausted the shotgun, he produced handguns from under his coat and continued firing.

Outside the building, the students scattered. Some slipped on the ice. Blood was everywhere.

Freshman Jillian Martinez had been near the teacher's lectern at the front of the room when she saw the gunman enter.

'All I saw was the flash of shooting,' she said. 'He pulled out his gun. He just started shooting at all the kids. He just started shooting at people, and I ran out of there as fast as I could. I ran all the way to the student centre. When I got there, I could still hear shooting.'

As the victims fled across campus, the panic of the lecture hall began to spread.

'Everything was crazy,' said 20-year-old sophomore Ryan Toms, who was trying to drive out of a parking lot near Cole Hall. 'There were people running down the roads trying to get away, and the roads were just jampacked with cars trying to get out, and so many police cars and ambulances and fire trucks trying to get in and there's people in the way.'

Widespread panic

NIU Police Chief Donald Grady said the department received a 911 call from inside the auditorium at 3.06pm. Police arrived 29 seconds later and found the gunman dead. He had shot himself.

Within minutes, the campus and DeKalb, a town of about 40,000 inhabitants, were jammed with traffic – with people trying to flee, while others flocked to the scene to find out if their loved ones were okay.

Stuck in traffic as she neared DeKalb from her home in nearby Park Ridge, Carolyn DeSantis fretted about the fate of her son, Michael, a freshman. Fear rose with each passing minute.

'I was just freaking out,' said DeSantis. 'I called him every five minutes to see if he was okay.'

Fortunately, he was not among the dead or injured.

Desiree Smith found refuge in a nearby campus building and called her parents and boyfriend. She was then told to go to an auditorium for questioning. There, she ran into the girl she had locked eyes with under the seats of the classroom.

'We ran to each other and hugged. I told her I kept thinking of her and wondering if she was okay,' Smith said. 'She said she kept thinking of me and that she remembered my face and remembered me grabbing on to her.'

The class teacher, Joseph Peterson, was also in the auditorium, despite being wounded.

'We were all relieved to see he was okay,' Smith said. 'I lost it and started crying then. I could see the horror and shock in his face.'

History of mental illness

The gunman had been armed with a Remington 870 shotgun and three handguns – a 9mm Glock, a 9mm Sig Sauer and a .380 Hi-Point – all legally owned. The police found 48 shell cases and six spent shotgun shells. A University of Illinois identification card in the name of post-grad student Stephen P Kazmierczak, a 27-year-old graduate of Northern Illinois University, was discovered in his pocket.

'There were no red flags,' said campus police chief, Donald Grady, the day after the shooting, adding that Kazmierczak was someone 'revered by faculty and students alike'.

His girlfriend, Jessica Baty, said that, during their two-year courtship, she had never seen him display violent tendencies and she expressed bewilderment over the cause of the rampage.

'He was anything but a monster,' Baty said. 'He was probably the nicest, most caring person ever.'

However, she confirmed that Kazmierczak was taking the anti-anxiety medication Xanax, sleep-aid Ambien and the anti-depressant Prozac, all of which were prescribed to him by a psychiatrist. She said that he stopped taking Prozac about three weeks prior to the 14 February shooting and, according to campus police, his behaviour had become 'somewhat erratic'.

Kazmierczak did have a history of mental illness. Born in Elk Grove Village, Illinois, on 26 August 1980, he was treated temporarily for mental illness at the Elk Grove Village Thresholds-Mary Hill House psychiatric centre after graduating from high school in 1998 for being 'unruly' at home, according to his parents. They put him into care.

He enlisted in the US Army in September 2001 and was discharged in February 2002 before completing basic training for lying on his application form about his mental illness. He went on to study Sociology at Northern Illinois University. Meanwhile, his parents moved to a retirement home in Florida in 2004. Two years later, his mother died.

Kazmierczak graduated from NIU in 2006, receiving the Dean's award and was considered a stand-out, well-regarded student. Campus police describe him as a 'fairly normal' and 'unstressed person'. NIU President, John G Peters, said that Kazmierczak had 'a very good academic record, no record of trouble'. He was Vice-President of the NIU chapter of the American Correctional Association and had written about the US correctional system, specifically prisons.

An 'extremely sensitive individual'

In 2006, Kazmierczak, along with two other graduate students and under the lead authorship of a sociology professor, had co-authored an academic paper entitled 'Self-injury in Correctional Settings: "Pathology of Prisons or of Prisoners?"' It was published in the academic journal, *Criminology & Public Policy*.

In the spring of 2007, he enrolled in an Arabic course at NIU and a course called 'Politics of the Middle East'. His research paper was on Hamas and its social service projects. That autumn, he moved as a graduate student in the School of Social Work at the University of Illinois at Urbana-Champaign, where he intended to study mental health issues. Meanwhile, he worked briefly at the Rockville Correctional Facility for Women near the Illinois–Indiana border, leaving after a couple of weeks without explanation. At the time of the shooting, he was enrolled full time at UIUC.

In his essays, he discussed being alienated from his parents when they put him into care.

'For as long as I can remember, I have always been an extremely sensitive individual and feel as though I am able to empathize with other people's emotional and social needs,' Kazmierczak wrote. 'However, some of my peers were not very understanding or accepting, and I feel as though I was victimized to a certain degree during my adolescent years.'

That victimization, he explained in an application to the University of Illinois School of Social Work, came from overwhelming social pressures.

'In hindsight, I feel that this was largely a result of the sensitivity that I often exhibited toward other classmates, which was not necessarily accepted by others,' Kazmierczak wrote.

Steven Kazmierczak – 'His face was blank, like he wasn't a person'.

He also talked about wanting to work with the mentally ill in the criminal justice system.

'I truly do feel as though I would be an altruistic social worker, mainly due to my past experiences, because I view myself as being able to relate to those segments of society that are in need of direction,' he wrote.

Four days before the shooting, he called his father, Robert.

'He was okay,' Robert Kazmierczak said. 'We made dinner plans. He was talking about the future.'

He told the *Chicago Tribune* that he and his wife, Gail, put Stephen into care for his own good.

'We did everything we could to help him. My wife and I worked very hard to help my son. I thought he was doing well,' Robert Kazmierczak said. 'He still had a lot of support. He knew I would help him if he was in trouble.'

Girlfriend Jessica Baty said that Kazmierczak had called her early on Valentine's Day to say goodbye and told her not to forget about him. Later, he killed five and wounded 18 before turning a gun on himself.

After the shooting, authorities intercepted a number of packages he had sent to Jessica, which included such items as a gun holster and ammunition, a textbook on serial killers, a book, *The Antichrist*, by Friedrich Nietzsche, and a final note written for her, signed with his full name.

The shooting was baffling to those who knew him, as he appeared outgoing and never appeared to have social problems. Some of Kazmierczak's former NIU roommates described him as a quiet man who usually kept himself to himself. They stated that, while fairly normal, they did not see him spend much time with other students.

However, in the article, 'Portrait of the School Shooter as a Young Man' published in *Esquire* magazine that July, it became clear he had a history of mental illness and attempted suicides, was bullied in high school and had shown an interest in previous school shootings, particularly those at Columbine High School and Virginia Tech. According to a report published by the United States Fire Administration, Kazmierczak is believed to have studied Seung-hui Cho's actions and adopted a similar MO.

CHAPTER 21

Isaac Zamora

2 September 2008

At 2.19pm on 2 September 2008, the police received a 911 call from Dennise Zamora, a resident of the small town of Alger in North Skagit County, Washington State. Deputy Anne Jackson was sent to investigate. She had had dealings with the Zamora family in the past and had told Dennise to call her any time she needed help.

Deputy Jackson arrived at the 19300 block of Bridle Place in Alger at 2.50pm. When she did not check in with her dispatchers, other deputies were sent to investigate. They found 40-year-old Jackson dead, alongside the corpse of a man. This was 58-year-old Chester Rose, whose house had been broken into, prompting Dennise to call the police.

At 4.10pm, the police received a call saying that the deputies were 'under fire'. Next, motorcyclist Ben Mercado was shot in the arm at a nearby Shell gas station. Officers identified the perpetrator and started a 26-km (16-mile) high-speed car chase south down Interstate 5. Shots were exchanged and 42-year-old Washington State Trooper, Troy Giddings, was shot in the arm, but he was able to drive himself to hospital in Sedro Woolley, 10 km (6 miles) from the interstate, where he was treated and released.

The police then received word of a fatal collision at mile post 238 near the Bow Hill Creek Road exit of I-5. They found an SUV on the central reserve. The driver, 64-year-old Leroy Lange, had been shot and killed.

Then, at 4.30pm, 28-year-old Isaac Zamora drove up to the sheriff's office in Mount Vernon, Washington, and turned himself in. He was the killer he said and his spree, it seemed, had come to an end. However, the full extent of his rampage was yet to be revealed.

At 5pm, one of Zamora's neighbours came home to find two workmen – David Radcliffe, 57, and Greg Gillum, 38 – dead in her house in the 1950 block of Silver Creek Road. Zamora had also stabbed 61-year-old Richard Treston, who had escaped and run for help. While the wounded man was being treated in hospital, the police found the dead body of 48-year-old Julie Binschus in his house. Her husband, Fred, had also suffered gunshot wounds. In all, six people were dead and four wounded.

Zamora had only been released from jail on 6 August, less than four weeks before the killings. His custodial sentence was to be followed by one year's community supervision. Zamora had been checking in to the Department of Corrections regularly and had passed drug and alcohol tests on 21 August.

Now, he was charged with 20 felony counts, including six counts of aggravated first-degree murder that could bring the death sentence. At his first hearing, Zamora mumbled 'guilty, guilty, guilty, guilty' as he entered.

'Can you hear me? I'm guilty,' he told Skagit County Superior Court.

However, public defender, Keith Tyne, said that it was clear that Zamora had significant mental health issues and he would defend him on that basis. But Zamora's mother Dennise did not want to hear any excuses made for her son.

'I'm not one of those people who say he's not guilty by reason of insanity,' she said. 'He is guilty by reason of insanity.'

A quiet, unremarkable kid

Born in 1980, there was little in Isaac Zamora's early life that indicated that he would become a psycho killer.

'I remember a sweet, sweet, sensitive mama's boy,' said Rachel Brown who grew up with him.

His mother cosseted him. She taught him at home, rather than sending him to school, while his father took him to Boy Scouts. Neighbour Christie Howard remembered him as a quiet, unremarkable kid. At worst, she recalls, he 'was one of the kids who rode his obnoxious motorcycle through the property.'

Then, when Zamora was about 14, the family home burned down and they lost everything. They struggled to cope both emotionally and financially.

'It's all we can do to keep the electricity on,' his mother wrote in the family's bankruptcy petition.

Zamora was deeply affected. A doctor diagnosed he was suffering from post-traumatic stress disorder and said that his problems would subside after puberty. They did not.

The family stayed in the neighbourhood, putting a large mobile home on the lot. Around the same time, Zamora stole his mother's gun to sell it to another teenager. He was later charged with filing a false report after telling police that a stranger had stolen it.

In 2001, Zamora and a friend were accused of stealing an outboard motor. Zamora refused to co-operate with the Mount Vernon Police Department, who were investigating the theft. But his mother got into his room by climbing through the window of the trailer, found the outboard motor and turned it over to police. Zamora pleaded guilty to second-degree theft and served three days in jail plus seven days' community service.

Voices in the head

Around 2000, Zamora met Connie Hickman when they were both working at a health-care facility.

'He was kind,' she said. 'He was easy to talk to, easy to get along with.'

They began going out, but he had trouble holding down jobs. He would make threats and start fights over things that never happened, Hickman said. Initially, she attributed this to Zamora's drinking and drug use. He was arrested for the possession of marijuana and cocaine.

After several suicide attempts, Zamora told Connie Hickman that he was hearing voices. In 2003, Hickman and Dennise Zamora took him to a Whatcom County hospital, saying they feared for their safety. He was diagnosed with both bipolar disorder and schizophrenia, and he was held there for several weeks before being discharged.

'The night after he was released, he called me and said: "I want to go back,"' Hickman said. But when he returned to the hospital, they refused to admit him.

Eventually, Zamora was admitted to another hospital. During that stay, court records show he bit an orderly who was trying to restrain him. Criminal charges were filed, then dropped.

'The next day, they discharged him,' Hickman recalled. 'How could they put him out on the streets when it was obvious the man had some issues?'

After being released, Zamora stopped taking his medication. He did not have a job and could not afford to pay for it. His behaviour became increasingly volatile. Hickman dropped him, changed her phone number and took out a protection order. But he was able to track her down through friends. One night, after she bumped into him on the street, a wine bottle came flying through her apartment window. On another occasion, the windscreen of her roommate's car was smashed.

Eventually Hickman fled the state, but he tracked her down, leaving rambling messages on relatives' answering machines. However, she managed to elude him. Meanwhile, his family tried to get him back into treatment. But his trouble with the law continued.

Friends said that, on good days, Zamora could be charming, warm and creative. But he could be strange, too. He would walk aimlessly around the streets alone at all hours or cause trouble by grabbing a fistful of paper towels from the gas station and letting them trail out of the window of his car as he drove off. More recently though, they said, he had become increasingly scary.

Killing for God

For ten years, he had shown signs of serious mental illness. Meanwhile, he racked up dozens of criminal charges. While none of them were for particularly violent offences, the state Department of Corrections had put

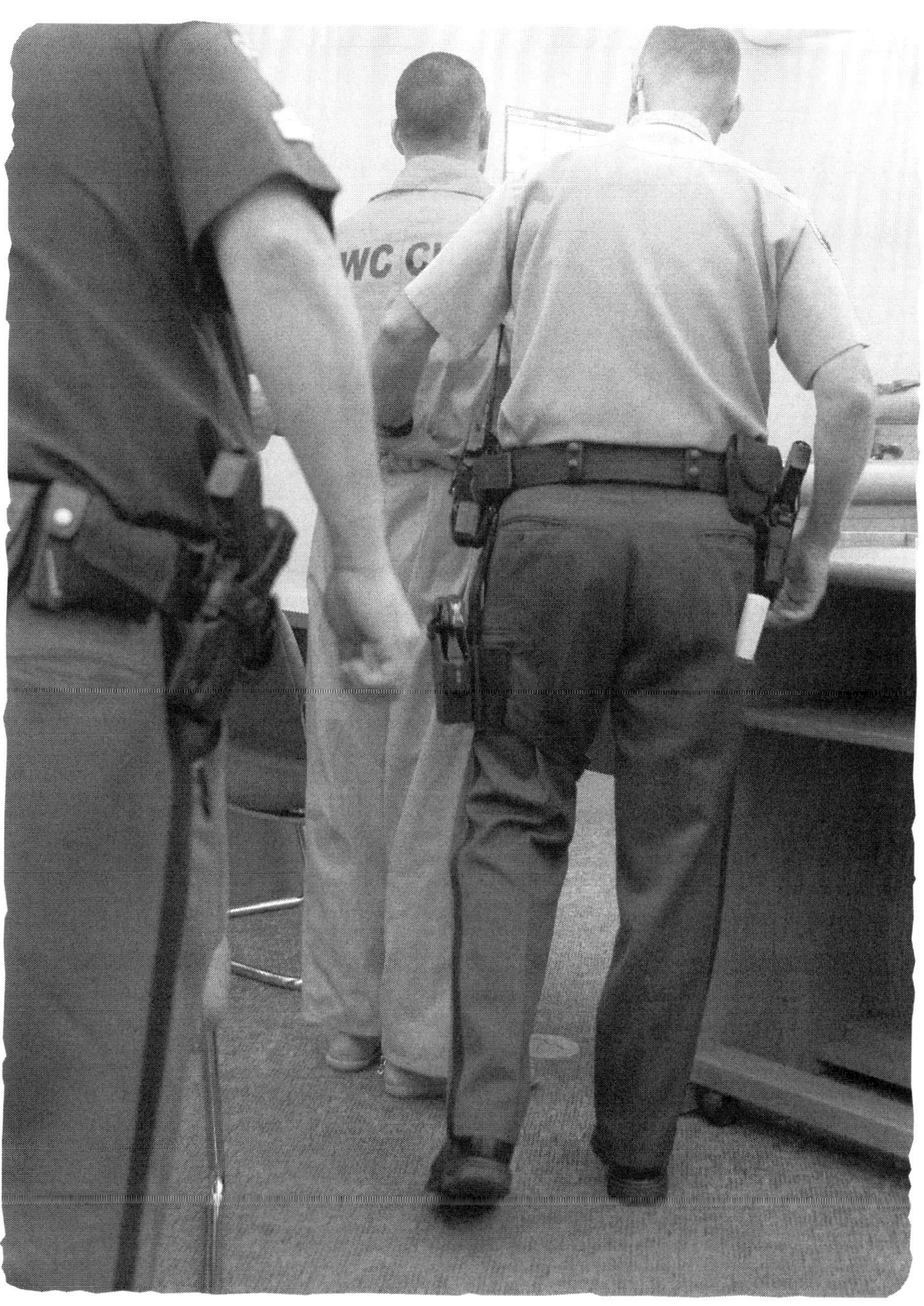

Isaac Zamora under arrest. He was described as 'devious and vengeful'.

him on a programme for offenders with mental illness. However, Zamora would not continue his mental health treatment, despite his family's urgings, and the law prevented them from forcing a 28-year-old to do so.

After he had been released from jail, his parents threw him out and he began sleeping in the woods, then on neighbours' lawns. The week before his murder spree, he told neighbour, Shirley Wenrick: 'I am going to get even with them.'

However, he agreed to take the first of two evaluations he needed to qualify for state mental health programmes. He received some treatment, but his mental problems continued. Symptoms ranged from suicide attempts to auditory hallucinations, from smashing windshields to outright threats.

In May 2007, he flew into a rage when a friend refused to go hiking with him and he hurled a concrete block at the friend's car, damaging it. Zamora was charged with second-degree malicious mischief. In a statement to Skagit County Court, the friend described Zamora as 'devious and vengeful'.

On 15 May, he pleaded guilty. As part of his sentencing, he agreed not to have firearms, although neighbours said he had a collection of six or seven guns. It transpired that the guns he used in his killing spree were stolen from a house near his mother's home.

On his release, he was supposed to undergo a mental health evaluation, but he did not have the money to pay for one. The Department of Corrections had to go to the state's Department of Social and Health Services for the money. All this took time and, by the time the first of his evaluations was scheduled, it was too late for Zamora and his victims.

Although he still had enough sense to hand himself in after the rampage, by the time he got to court his condition had deteriorated further. At a second hearing on 5 September, he said: 'I kill for God. I listen to God.'

Under 24-hour guard

Puzzlingly, he pleaded guilty on four counts of aggravated first-degree murder and six counts of attempted first-degree murder to avoid the death penalty, but not guilty by reason of insanity for two others. He also pleaded guilty on eight other charges.

'I accepted the plea bargain because I was afraid I would be sentenced to death, and would ultimately be executed if I went to trial and was unable to convince a jury I was insane at the time of the crimes,' Zamora wrote in a declaration.

His attorney told the court that Zamora had been diagnosed with schizophrenia on several occasions. A doctor then testified that Zamora thought he was shooting demons that day.

He was confined at Western State Hospital and put under 24-hour guard by two Department of Corrections SWAT team members and one employee of Washington State's Department of Social and Health Services because of his apparent threats to escape, as well as threats against individuals working at the hospital and against the community at large. Two psychiatrists there maintained that he was not mentally ill, but psychopathic because he bragged about the people he had killed.

In 2017, he was transferred from the state mental hospital to prison to foil a planned escape attempt. His mother was concerned.

'He met this silly girl and they wrote to each other, tripping like crazy people do, about how they would escape,' said Dennise Zamora. 'I can't blame the institution for being concerned, but he doesn't know what he's doing. When did it become OK to send a severely mentally ill person to prison?'

Two years later, Zamora sought to withdraw his guilty pleas and petitioned for a new trial. His petition was denied.

CHAPTER 22

Anthony Sowell

2007-2009

Known in the press as The Cleveland Strangler, Anthony Sowell, then aged 50, was arrested in October 2009 as a suspect in the murders of 11 women, whose bodies were discovered in and around his duplex in the Mount Pleasant neighbourhood of Cleveland, Ohio.

For two years, it had been noted that, on hot days, the stench surrounding the 12200 block of Cleveland's Imperial Avenue could be unbearable. It was the smell of something decomposing. Some thought the sewers had backed up; others rudely attributed the odour to Ray's Sausage factory, one of the few businesses still flourishing in that rundown area of the city's East Side. Zack Reed, a local councillor whose mother lived a block away, said that he called the city health department in 2007 after a resident complained about something that smelled 'like a dead body'. The sewers were flushed, but the stink did not go away.

On 22 September 2009, Anthony Sowell invited a woman he knew back to the home he rented at 12205 Imperial to share four bottles of cheap malt liquor he had. She was perhaps unaware that Sowell was a registered sex offender with a long history of abuse behind him.

Difficult background

Sowell was one of seven siblings born to Claudia 'Gertrude' Garrison. When his older sister died, her seven children came to live with their Aunt Gertrude, who was a martinet. His niece testified that Garrison would force her and her twin sister to strip naked in front of the other children, tie them to the banister and whip them with an electrical cord until they bled, while Sowell looked on.

'It was psycho,' she said.

She also said that, when she was ten, Sowell, then 12, and the other males in the household would rape her almost daily. Unable to tell his school friends about this, they continually ribbed him for being a virgin.

At the age of 18, Sowell joined the US Marine Corps and served seven years. He was discharged in 1985 with a Good Conduct Medal and letters of commendation. While he was in the service, he married a woman who sought to curb his excessive drinking. They had a child, but she divorced him the day he left the Marines.

He returned to Cleveland, where he continued drinking heavily, clocking up a record for disorderly conduct, public drunkenness, driving under the influence, domestic violence and drug possession. Cleveland was undergoing an epidemic of crack at the time.

In 1989, Sowell repeatedly raped a 21-year-old woman, who was three months pregnant. She had gone to Sowell's home on Page Avenue voluntarily, she later told police, but when she tried to leave, he bound her hands and feet with a tie and a belt and gagged her with a rag. The victim told officers: 'He choked me real hard because my body started tingling. I thought I was going to die.'

When Sowell fell asleep, she wriggled free. Sowell was indicted by a grand jury but did not turn up in court. Seven months later and 6 km (4 miles) away, a 31-year-old woman, who was five months pregnant, said Sowell raped her, too. She had gone home with him for a drink.

Suddenly, he started choking her and abusing her with a stream of obscenities. Then he raped her orally, vaginally and anally, though she begged him to stop. According to the police report, Sowell forced her to say: 'Yes, sir, I like it.'

Again, she escaped when he fell asleep. She returned in the morning with the police and he was arrested. But no charges were filed as, later, she could not be found to testify. However, the police now had their man for the first rape. He was sentenced to 15 years.

Registered sex offender

In prison, he signed up with Alcoholics Anonymous, but was turned down for a treatment course as he would not admit that he was a sexual offender. Otherwise, he was a model prisoner. However, fellow prisoner, Carlton Pope, said: 'I shunned him because not only did he seem demented and a psychotic pervert, he carried the stigma of a convicted rapist.'

Although he passed other courses, he was denied early release and served his full term. Apparently clean and sober, a psychological evaluation deemed him unlikely to rape again. Nevertheless, he had to register as a sex offender and report to the local sheriff's office once a year until a 2008 federal law mandated that he had to check in every 90 days.

Anthony Sowell, the Cleveland Strangler.

When he left prison in 2005, Sowell moved to the crime-ridden district of East Cleveland. He lived there with his stepmother until she was hospitalized in 2007, and he often blamed the smell on her.

An agency for ex-offenders got him a job as a rubber moulder at the Custom Rubber Corp and he took on the role as 'helper' to local women who prostituted themselves for a rock of crack, plying them with malt liquor and sometimes providing shelter. He was perfectly positioned to entertain them as his disabled stepmother could not climb the stairs to his third-floor apartment. Some reported that, after he had befriended them, he turned on them.

According to his then girlfriend, Tanja Doss, he was not using crack cocaine himself at the time. They drank beer, played chess and barbecued. He told Doss he had been in prison but that he had taken the rap for a crime committed by someone else.

'He seemed like a regular human being,' she said. But 'he had little laughter in him.'

Others found him 'not crazy, but strange. Sort of quiet, mousy, sneaky, sort of.'

Around that time, he set up an account with the fetish website Alt.com, saying that he was a 'master' looking for a 'submissive'. He was also having a relationship with Lori Frazier, the niece of Cleveland Mayor, Frank Jackson. A crackhead, she lived with him from 2005 to 2007. During that time, he would lure other women off the street, offering them alcohol or drugs. Some were assaulted, but when they reported this to police, little was done. Others did not escape.

In May or June 2007, 38-year-old Crystal Dozier disappeared. She was the mother of seven children. Her family reported her missing to the police, but it was not the first time she had gone missing, so they made little effort to investigate.

It was around then that the stink started. The owner of the sausage factory spent $20,000 on new pipework and waste systems. It passed the necessary health inspections, but the factory workers kept the windows closed to keep out the stench.

Losing his marbles

When Sowell split up with Frazier, his life began to fall apart. He lost his job and supported himself by pushing a shopping trolley around town, collecting scrap metal. According to Doss, Sowell remained obsessed with Frazier and kept some of her clothes. By then, he too was smoking crack. This was particularly dangerous when mixed with heavy drinking and marijuana.

In December 2008, Gladys Wade waved down a police car. She was covered in blood. She told officers that Sowell had invited her in for a beer; when she had refused, he dragged her upstairs and choked her until she passed out. When she came round, she found that he had stripped her naked and was trying to rape her. She escaped and fled to a nearby restaurant and begged the customers to call 911. They told her to use the payphone outside.

Sowell was arrested, but he maintained that he had caught Gladys trying to rob his house. The police told Wade that it was only her word against his and he was released. He would claim at least another five victims before he was arrested again in 2009.

In April 2009, Sowell turned on his former girlfriend, Tanja Doss, after she agreed to go to Sowell's house for a beer. She knew he had been in prison, but did not know why. Once he got her home, he tried to strangle her. Pinning her to the floor, he told her to knock three times if she wanted to live. Otherwise, no one would miss her.

She knocked. He released her and made her strip, but they had both drunk so much that they passed out. In the morning, he let her go, offering her money, food and clothing as he had in other cases. She did not report the incident to the police because of an outstanding drugs charge. Later that month, her best friend, 43-year-old Nancy Cobbs, disappeared, another of Sowell's victims. Even then, she did not suspect Sowell until he was arrested.

As a registered sex offender, he was required to report regularly to the sheriff's department. Officers had visited his house on 22 September, but did not have the power to enter. Only a few hours after their visit, Sowell and a woman companion went upstairs to a room that contained only a chair, a blanket and an extension cord. After they had had a few drinks, Sowell became angry. He punched her in the face and began choking her with the cord. When she passed out, he raped her. She managed to get away by promising not to go to the police and he gave her $50.

She went to the hospital the following day, then spoke to the police. An investigator was assigned to the case, but it took the police several weeks to obtain a search warrant.

Soon after, neighbours saw a naked woman fall from a second-storey window. When the casualty was taken to hospital, she was found to be under the influence of drugs and she refused to speak to the police.

House of horrors

Meanwhile Fawcett Bess, who owned Bess Chicken and Pizza across the road from the sausage factory, had talked to a woman who said that Sowell had attacked her and showed him bruises that she said he had inflicted. Then, in October, he saw Sowell naked in the bushes outside his house. He was beating a naked woman. Bess called 911. The ambulance came to take the woman to hospital. The police turned up hours later, but did not even talk to Sowell who was in the house at the time.

The police returned to Sowell's home on 29 October 2009 with an arrest warrant for the alleged rape. He was not there, but this time the officers had obtained a search warrant. They found two bodies on the living room floor; two more bodies were discovered in a crawl space under the house, another in a shallow grave in the basement and a sixth in a freshly dug grave in the back garden. A heated tent was erected over the disturbed soil, so that the forensic crews digging up the backyard could work at night. Three more bodies were then found to have been buried there. A human skull was also found in a bucket inside the house, bringing the body count to 11.

The police came in for heavy criticism for not having caught Sowell sooner. His victims were Black and poor; most were homeless or lived alone, with histories of drug and alcohol abuse. Because of these circumstances, their families said, the police disregarded them as missing persons' cases.

Sowell was charged with murder, rape and kidnapping. The Cleveland police reopened the files of other women who had gone missing in the area. In the 1980s, two women's bodies had been found in an abandoned building on First Avenue. Both had been strangled and one of them was living near Sowell on Page Avenue. A third woman was found strangled in her home around the corner in Hayden Avenue. Two of them were thought to be drug-users.

The police were convinced that there were more bodies out there. A dumpster behind Sowell's house was giving off a dreadful stench, and Sowell had been seen dragging large garbage bags down the street. The police dug up the rest of his garden and that of the house next door.

In all, Sowell faced 85 counts of murder, rape and kidnapping. He initially pleaded not guilty by reason of insanity, which he later changed to a simple not guilty. He was convicted of all but two charges against him.

In an unsworn statement, Sowell told the jury: 'The only thing I want to say is I'm sorry. I know that might not sound like much, but I truly am sorry from the bottom of my heart.'

They didn't buy it. He was sentenced to death, but died in prison of a terminal illness in 2021 before the sentence could be carried out.

CHAPTER 23

Jiverly Antares Wong

3 April 2009

In November 2008, 41-year-old Jiverly Antares Wong – aka Jiverly Voong – walked into an employment centre in downtown Binghamton, upstate New York. He had been laid off from his job at a vacuum cleaner plant, and he needed help applying for unemployment benefits.

A naturalized American citizen, he spoke only broken English and the receptionist offered him a phone number that he could call in Chinese or Japanese.

'I'm Vietnamese!' he told her, before turning around and storming out.

Nevertheless, he managed to get his unemployment benefit of $200 a week and it was suggested that he take English lessons to improve his chances of getting a job.

Cold-hearted killer

He had an appointment back at the employment centre at 10am on 3 April 2009, but did not show up. Half-an-hour later, he blocked the rear door of the American Civic Association immigration centre, where he had been taking classes, with a vehicle registered in his father's name.

Wearing a bullet-proof vest covered by a bright green nylon jacket, Wong then entered the building through the front door, shooting at anyone who stood in his path. Without saying a word, he went up to the reception desk and shot one of the Civic Association's receptionists through the head, killing her. He shot the other receptionist, Shirley DeLucia, in the stomach. She feigned death. When the gunman moved on, she took cover under a desk and called 911. The call was logged at 10.38am. She then stayed on the line for 39 minutes and relayed information until she was rescued.

Wong walked into an English language class, just off the main reception area, and continued shooting. Everyone who was in that classroom suffered a gunshot wound. When Wong heard the police sirens, he turned the gun on himself and took his own life. In a matter of minutes, he had fired 99 rounds; 88 from a 9mm Beretta and 11 from a .45-calibre Beretta, killing 13 of his fellow immigrants.

Among the wounded was 42-year-old Vietnamese immigrant, Long Huynh, who had tried to shield his wife, Lan Ho, but a bullet that shattered Huynh's elbow ricocheted, striking his wife and killing her. He said later that he wished he had died, too, and only continued to live for the sake of their two children.

When the police arrived, they did not know whether the gunman was alive or dead. They locked down nearby Binghamton High School and a number of surrounding streets. Learning that the perpetrator was Vietnamese, they called in Broome Community College assistant, professor Tuong Hung Nguyen, who was fluent in the language.

A SWAT team was sent in and began clearing the building at 11.13am. Even then, they had to proceed with caution as Wong's suicide had not been confirmed. A number of people had taken refuge in a closet in the basement, and it was feared that the gunman had taken hostages. It was not until after 12 noon that Wong was found dead from a self-inflicted gunshot wound in an office on the first floor of the building.

He had been carrying two semi-automatic Berettas that matched the serial numbers on his New York State pistol licence. A hunting knife was found tucked in his waistband and a bag of ammunition was tied around his neck. A number of unspent magazines was also found at the scene, along with a laser sight.

An unhappy life

Wong's sister said that she had no idea that her brother was going to go on the rampage. They did not live together, but she spoke to him on the phone at least once a week. However, those who knew him better were not surprised.

'From the people close to him, this action he took was not a surprise to them,' said Binghamton Police Chief, Joseph Zikuski. 'Apparently, people were making fun of him. He felt degraded by his inability to speak English and he was upset about that.'

Jiverly Antares Wong was an outsider. He was a Hoa – that is, an ethnic Chinese inhabitant of Vietnam. For centuries, Chinese emperors used Vietnam as a place of exile. His father had fought alongside the Americans in the South Vietnamese Army during the Vietnam War. The family had come to America. Wong had lived in New York, California and, briefly, Canada. He naturalized in the US in 1995. In Los Angeles, he worked for seven years as a delivery man for the catering company, Kikka Sushi. During his time there, he married, though he never told his family. The couple later divorced. He also picked up a misdemeanour conviction for passing a bad cheque. After he moved to Binghamton, Wong worked at a local Shop-Vac vacuum-cleaner plant.

Wong was unhappy. He had allegedly made comments such as 'America sucks'. Asked who he was going to vote for in the presidential election, he said: 'I don't really care. I'd shoot both of them.'

He had recently lost his job when the plant closed in November 2008 and was having difficulties finding another one.

However, one of his former co-workers told CNN: 'He was quiet – not a violent person… I can't believe he would do something like this.'

At the same time, his girlfriend left him. A colleague said: 'Maybe she loves your money.' He just smiled. Short of money, he moved back in with his parents.

It seems, he had been planning the attack for some time. He had had a licence to own a handgun since June 1997 and, after he moved to Binghamton, he signed up with two shooting ranges for target practice. A man occupying a neighbouring lane said: 'He was basically shooting his shots

A police officer walks out of Jiverly Wong's house.

in rapid succession with virtually no hesitation between shots, very smooth and steady and rapid shooting.'

He claimed to have fired some 10,000 rounds in a year. Though others found him pleasant, clearly his paranoia was growing, believing that law enforcement agencies were out to get him.

Paranoid statement

A few days after the incident, an envelope was delivered to News 10 Now, a TV station in Syracuse, upstate New York. It was dated 18 March 2009, but postmarked 3 April 2009, the day of the shootings. The envelope contained photos of Wong, smiling and holding his guns, as well as a gun permit, Wong's driver's licence and a two-page handwritten letter largely in capital letters. It read:

DATE: MARCH - 18 - 2009
DEAR: NEW TEN NOW
I AM JiVERLY WONG SHOOTING THE PEOPLE
THE FiRST I WANT TO SAY SORRY I KNOW A LiTTLE ENGLiSH I HOPE YOU UNDERSTAND ALL OF THiS. OF COURSE YOU NEED TO KNOW WHY I SHOOTING? BECAUSE UNDERCOVER COP GAVE ME A LOT OF ASS DURiNG EiGHTEEN YEARS. I GOT SEVEN YEARS AND EiGHT MONTH DELiVERY TO GROCERY IN THE CALiFORNiA. CAME BACK NEW YORK ON THE AUGUST – 2007. LET TALK ABOUT WHEN I LiVE IN CALiFORNiA. SUCH AS... COP USED 24 HOURS THE TECHNiQUE OF ULTRAMODERN AND CAMERA FOR BURN THE CHEMiCAL IN MY HOUSE. FOR SWiTCH THE CHANNEL Ti.Vi. FOR ADJUST THE FAN. FOR MADE ME UNBREATHBLE. FOR MADE ME VOMiT. FOR CONNECT THE MUSiC INTO MY EAR.

UNDERCOVER COP USUAL COiNED SOME NASTY WAS NOT TRUE ABOUT ME AND SPREAD A RUMOUR TO THE RECEiVER AND SOME PEOPLE KNOW ME CONDUCE TOWARD MANY PEOPLE PREJUDiCED AND SELFiSH TO ME... COP MADE ME LOST MY JOB... COP PUT ME BECAME POOR.

LET TALK ABOUT WHEN I LiVE AT THE 28.BAKER . ST. 2ND FLOOR. JOHNSON CiTY. NEW YORK 13790. IT TERRiBLE WHEN I LiVE THERE SUCH AS... COP WAiT UNTiL MiDNiGHT WHEN I OFF THE LiGHT AND WENT TO THE BED. COP UNLOCK MY DOOR AND CAME IN TAKE A SiT IN MY ROOM <<COP DiD IT THiRTEEN TiME ON THE YEAR 1994>> ON THE THiRTEEN TiME HAD

THREE TiME TOUCH ME WHEN I SLEEPiNG. ONE TiME STOLEN 20 DOLLAR IN MY WALLET ONE TiME USED ELECTRiC GUN SHOOT AT THE BEHiND MY NECK. (THAT TiME I DiD NOT KNOW ENGLiSH)

PLEASE CONTiNUE SECOND PAGE THANK YOU.

[Page 2]

FROM 1990 TO 1995 NEW YORK UNDERCOVER COP TRY TO GET A CAR ACCiDENT WiTH ME. SUCH AS WHEN I DRiViNG ON THE HiGHWAY AND ON THE STREET UNDERCOVER COP SUNDDENLY BRAKE THE CAR STOP IMMEDiATELY AT THE OF FRONT MY CAR . . . COP DiD IT 32 TiME LiKE THAT DURiNG 1990 TO 1995 BUT I NEVER HiT THE CAR.

MANY TiME FROM 1990 TO 1997 AT THE DAY TiME . . . COP EXPLOiT UNKNON ENGLiSH AND WENT TO MY HOUSE KNOCK THE DOOR FOR HARASS AND DOMiNEER. OF COURSE DURiNG THAT TiME COP COiNED SOMETHiNG WAS NOT TRUE ABOUT ME AND SPREAD A RUMOUR NASTY LiKE THE CALiFORNiA COP.

FROM AUGUST – 2007 UNTiL NOW COP GAVE ME NOT TO MUCH ASS ONLY ONE TiME COP LEAVE A MASSAGE IN MY VOiCE MAiL AND SAiD << COME BACK YOUR COUNTRY >> AFTER FIVE MiNUTE I SEND A TEXT MASSAGE TO THEM I SAiD I WILL CALL THE POLiCE AND THEY SEND IT BACK TO ME THEY SAiD THEY ARE THE POLiCE

DEAR. NEW TEN NOW. RiGHT NOW I STiLL GET UNEMPLOMENT BENEFiT OF THE COMPANY SHOP VAC ENDiCOTT. NEW YORK STATE DEPARTMENT OF

LABOR WAS CHEAT AND UNPAiD FROM DECEMBER – 1st – 2008 TO DECEMBER – 28th – 2008. I ALREADY CLAiM WEEKLY BENEFiT FROM THAT DATE. ANY WAY I CAN NOT ACCEPTED MY POOR LiFE. BEFORE I CUT MY POOR LiFE I MUST ONESELF GET A JUDGE JOB FOR MAKE AN IMPARTiAL WiTH UNDERCOVER COP BY AT LEAST TWO PEOPLE WiTH ME GO TO RETURN TO THE DUST OF EARTH.

ALREADY IMPARTiAL NOW… COP BRiNG ABOUT THiS SHOOTiNG COP MUST RESPONSiBLE. AND YOU HAVE A NiCE DAY.

CHAPTER 24

Nidal Malik Hasan

5 November 2009

With the attack on New York's World Trade Center and the Pentagon on 11 September 2001, a new madness gripped the world. America was on the alert for attacks from abroad but also feared domestic terrorism.

One incident that particularly touched a nerve in America was the massacre at Fort Hood on 5 November 2009, when US Army psychiatrist Nidal Malik Hasan shot a number of soldiers who were about to be deployed in Iraq and Afghanistan. After the attack, the US Senate released a report describing the mass shooting as 'the worst terrorist attack on US soil since September 11, 2001'.

A Muslim of Palestinian descent, Hasan had expressed radical beliefs and had connections to Anwar al-Awlaki, a recruiter for al-Qaeda, who had preached to at least three of the 9/11 terrorists. An investigation conducted by the FBI concluded that his emails with the late Imam Anwar al-Awlaki were related to his authorized professional research and that he was not a threat.

However, he had expressed approval of the drive-by shootings of Carlos Leon Bledsoe in Little Rock, Arkansas, on 1 June 2009. Bledsoe had spent 16 months teaching in Yemen and had changed his name to Abdulhakim Mujahid Muhammad. He claimed to be a soldier with al-Qaeda in the Arabian Peninsula. Charged with capital murder, attempted capital murder and ten counts of unlawful discharge of a weapon, his lawyers defended him on the grounds that he suffered 'a delusional disorder'. But during the trial, Bledsoe changed his plea to guilty and was sentenced to life imprisonment without parole.

Conflicted individual

Nidal Malik 'AbduWali' Hasan was born in 1970 in Arlington, Virginia, to Palestinian parents who emigrated from the West Bank. He joined the US Army from high school. He served eight years as an enlisted soldier while attending college. After graduating from Virginia Tech in 1995 with a bachelor's degree in Biochemistry, he went to medical school, becoming an MD in 2003. He then completed a residency in psychiatry at the Walter Reed Army Medical Center.

In June 2007, at the culmination of his residency, he was supposed to make a presentation on a medical topic of his choosing. Instead, he gave a talk called 'The Koranic World View as it Relates to Muslims in the US Military'.

'It's getting harder and harder for Muslims in the service to morally justify being in a military that seems constantly engaged against fellow Muslims,' he said, and to avoid 'adverse events', the military should allow Muslim soldiers to be released as conscientious objectors instead of fighting in wars against other Muslims. He made references to Osama bin Laden, the Taliban, suicide bombers and Iran and his final bullet point was: 'We love death more than you love life.' The talk was not well received.

His cousin said that Hasan was harassed by his fellow soldiers because of his religion. In August 2009, his car was vandalized – neighbours said it was because he was a Muslim. It was part of Hasan's job to offer counselling to those returning from Iraq and Afghanistan. The stories he heard turned him against those wars. Hasan himself was due to be sent to Afghanistan on 28 November and the soldiers he attacked were preparing to go overseas.

What should have alerted the authorities was Hasan's connections to radical preacher Anwar al-Awlaki, who has been described as the 'bin Laden of the internet'. Nidal Malik Hasan attended his sermons, along with three of the 9/11 hijackers. Al-Awlaki left the US in 2004 and moved to London, where it is thought he had contact with Umar Farouk Abdulmutallab, the suspect in the Northwest Airlines Flight terrorist attack over Detroit on

Christmas Day 2009. In 2004, he moved to Yemen. He was arrested in 2006 but released after 18 months. By December 2009, he was back on the Yemeni government's most-wanted list.

Between December 2008 and June 2009, US intelligence intercepted 18 emails between Hasan and al-Awlaki. In one, Hasan wrote: 'I can't wait to join you [in the afterlife].'

After the Fort Hood shooting, al-Awlaki praised Hasan as a hero. He said: 'Nidal opened fire on soldiers who were on their way to be deployed to Iraq and Afghanistan. How can there be any dispute about the virtue of what he has done? In fact, the only way a Muslim could Islamically justify serving as a soldier in the US army is if his intention is to follow in the footsteps of men like Nidal.'

Crazed rampage

At the time, Hasan was working at the Soldier Readiness Center at Fort Hood, where military personnel received routine medical checks before a deployment and immediately on their return. On 5 November 2009, he arrived at work around 1.20pm and took a seat at an empty table. Hasan bowed his head for several seconds and then he jumped on to a desk and shouted: '*Allahu Akbar*!' – 'God is great' – before producing two pistols. One of them was a FN Herstal 'Five-seven' semi-automatic pistol, which one firearms website describes as capable of defeating 'most body armour in military service around the world today'. He had bought it in a civilian store. The other was a .357 Magnum revolver, which he held in reserve.

The shots came so rapidly that Private First Class Marquest Smith, who was going over some paperwork in a cubicle in the building, said he thought at first the sound was microwave popcorn. Then someone shouted: 'Gun!'

Private Smith dived under a desk. He stayed there for several long minutes, before making a dash for safety. As he broke for the door, he saw Major Hasan in combat fatigues, moving around the room. His handgun was pointed downwards and he was methodically shooting the soldiers who were already on the ground or were crouching down, seeking cover. As Private Smith fled, a bullet hit his boot. It stuck in the sole, but he was uninjured. Army reserve captain John Gaffaney, who was unarmed, attempted to stop Hasan by charging at him and throwing a chair, but he was shot and mortally wounded.

Hasan moved on to fire at the crowd that had gathered for a college graduation ceremony scheduled in a nearby theatre. He appeared to focus on soldiers in uniform and fired more than 100 rounds. Although they were on an army base, none of the soldiers were armed. However, Kimberly Munley, a 35-year-old police officer, happened to be nearby. She was waiting for her squad car to get a tune-up when she heard the commotion and raced to the scene.

As she rounded a corner, she saw Major Hasan chasing a wounded soldier through an open courtyard as though he was trying to finish him off.

'He looked extremely focused,' said Francisco De La Serna, a 23-year-old medic who had fled the building.

Sergeant Munley's first shot missed Major Hasan. He spun to face her. The two of them then had a running gun battle. Munley took two bullets to her legs. Both entered her left thigh, ripped through the flesh and lodged in her right thigh. She also received a minor wound to the right wrist.

By then, a 911 call had been put in and Sergeant Mark Todd, another civilian police officer, arrived and fired at Hasan.

'He was firing at people as they were trying to run and hide,' said Todd. 'Then he turned and fired a couple of rounds at me. I didn't hear him say a word, he just turned and fired.'

Hasan was felled by shots from Todd, who then kicked a pistol out of Hasan's hand, and placed him in handcuffs as he fell unconscious.

Specialist De La Serna, who had taken cover across the street, sprinted to the scene as the shooting stopped and put a tourniquet on Munley, who faded in and out of consciousness. Then he moved to Hasan, who had a gunshot wound to the chest. Hasan was calm and quiet, and conscious but weak. He had a handgun at his side and the pockets of his combat fatigues were full of pistol magazines.

As soon as the shooting stopped, soldiers in the processing centre shifted into combat mode, ripping up their uniforms to use as tourniquets. The wounded flooded the emergency room on base, where nurses and doctors struggled to cope with the injuries.

Munley was rushed to hospital and underwent surgery to halt the bleeding that night. Her husband, a soldier stationed at Fort Bragg, flew in and her Twitter account filled with messages from people world-wide.

The incident had lasted about ten minutes. It resulted in more than 30 people being wounded and 13 killed – 12 soldiers and one civilian. Eleven died at the scene; two died later in hospital. The dead included at least one teenager, 19-year-old Aaron Nemelka, who joined the Army the previous year, straight out of high school, 22-year-old Specialist, Jason Dean Hunt, who had just married, and Francheska Velez, 21-year-old oil-tank driver who had completed tours in Korea and Iraq and who was two months pregnant with her first child when she died. Five Army reservists were also killed, including Michael Cahill, who was 62 and worked at the processing centre as a physician's assistant.

Unanimous verdict

Hasan was taken to Brooke Army Medical Center in Fort Sam Houston, Texas, where he was held under heavy guard. He was hit by at least four shots and paralyzed. Two weeks later, it was announced that eight of the wounded service-members would still be deployed overseas.

Controversially, the Army decided not to charge Hasan with terrorism. Rather, he was charged with 13 counts of premeditated murder, and 32 counts of attempted premeditated murder. Initially, he refused to enter a plea, though he admitted that he had done the shooting. The proceedings were muddied over the issue of whether he could be forcibly shaved to comply with US Army regulations.

Nidal Hasan: 'We love death more than you love life.'

He sought to conduct his own defence, but did not cross-examine the prosecution witnesses, called no witnesses for the defence and declined to testify in his own defence or make a closing statement.

A jury panel of 13 officers convicted him on all charges and unanimously recommended he be dismissed from the service and sentenced to death. Hasan was incarcerated at the United States Disciplinary Barracks at Fort Leavenworth, Kansas, awaiting execution, convinced that he would become a martyr.

CHAPTER 25

Ibrahim Shkupolli

31 December 2009

While students shoot their classmates in schools and universities, older gunmen choose shopping malls for their massacres. This also applies in Finland, which has developed a reputation for its spree killing.

On 31 December 2009, 43-year-old Ibrahim Shkupolli discovered that his ex-girlfriend had a lover in the grocery store where she worked in the Sello Prisma hypermarket in the Leppävaara district of Espoo, Finland's second-largest city, 21 km (13 miles) west of Helsinki. First, he brutally stabbed her to death in her apartment, then headed to the mall. There were between 2,000 and 3,000 people shopping there at the time.

Dressed in the black outfit favoured by crazed killers, Shkupolli arrived at the Prisma hypermarket at 10.08am. He went up to the second floor and opened fire with a 9mm handgun. Then, he moved down to the first floor, continuing his killing spree. He killed three men and one woman, all employees of Prisma. It is thought that his ex-girlfriend's lover was among the victims and had been shot twice in the head. The female victim was shot twice in the stomach, the men in the head. The ages of the victims were 27, 40, 42 and 45. Shkupolli then disappeared and the police began a major manhunt.

'There were loads of people who were crying, and many salespeople who were completely panicked,' a witness said.

A woman told a news reporter that she had seen the suspect carrying a long-barrelled pistol, rushing past the cashier line at the hypermarket, where the slayings took place. Another witness said he saw one worker lying on the floor covered in blood.

Hundreds of shop workers were evacuated to a nearby library and fire station, and the mall was cordoned off. Trains were halted at nearby

Leppävaara railway station and helicopters were brought in as police scoured the area.

Several hours later, Shkupolli was found dead in an apartment in Kirstinmäki, Espoo, where he had apparently committed suicide. His apartment was completely empty except for a mattress, a framed photo of his ex-girlfriend and 14 fully loaded magazines for his gun, together with a bag containing another 273 cartridges.

Later, the police went to his ex-girlfriend's flat and found her body. She was 32. Investigators said they believed that there was a 'domestic' motive for her murder. It seems she had taken out a restraining order against Shkupolli.

'The four victims in the shopping centre were, in a way, outsiders,' said Chief Inspector, Jukka Kaski. 'It looks like the incident is linked to the fifth victim. She seems to have been the gunman's main target and the whole shooting is tied up with the relationship between her and the gunman.'

Ibrahim Shkupolli proudly displaying the Albanian flag.

Restraining order

Born in Mitrovica, Kosovo, in 1966, Shkupolli was an Albanian who moved to Finland in 1990 when Kosovan autonomy was suppressed by Serbian leader and convicted war criminal Slobodan Milošević. For 28 years, he maintained a relationship with a Finnish girl, both before and after his marriage to an Albanian woman, who bore him three children. Shkupolli had a job in a warehousing company, organizing deliveries to the Prisma shop. His employer said he did not notice anything out of the usual in his behaviour prior to the shootings.

However, his girlfriend had filed charges about his behaviour. She claimed that he had threatened to kill her. The courts had imposed a restraining order, banning him from approaching her or her workplace. He had been convicted of assault and of possessing a handgun and ammunition, as well as narcotics. He was also under investigation for human trafficking from the Balkans to Finland and his application for Finnish citizenship had been rejected. The head of the Asylum Unit of the Finnish Immigration Service, Esko Repo, said his application for Finnish citizenship had been refused and he should have been deported.

Finland – with a population of 5.3 million – has 1.6 million firearms in private hands. The country has a deep-rooted hunting tradition and ranks, along with the United States at number one, among the top ten nations in the world for civilian gun ownership. The incident was Finland's third major shooting in two years. Again, politicians, social workers and religious leaders urged tighter gun laws and increased vigilance over internet sites. There have also been calls for more social cohesion in the small Nordic nation, known for its high suicide rate, heavy drinking and domestic violence.

After another school shooting just 15 months previously, the Finnish government had already announced that handgun permits would no longer be granted to first-time applicants. Instead, would-be gun owners must train for at least a year at a gun club before being allowed to apply for a permit. All applicants must also provide a note from a doctor giving them a clean bill of mental health and submit to being interviewed by the police. However, the gun Shkupolli used in his shooting spree was unlicensed.

According to a large-scale survey of the mental health of Kosovo Albanians living in Sweden by the Karolinska Institute in Stockholm, many suffered from clinical depression and post-traumatic stress disorder. Similar findings have been made in other countries that took large numbers of Bosnian or Kosovan refugees during and after the Balkan wars. There seems to have been no follow-up study in Finland, which has been one of the strongest champions of an independent Kosovan state. But Shkupolli does not appear to have ever been seen by a mental health professional.

CHAPTER 26

Christopher Speight

19 January 2010

Crazed gunmen do not always kill strangers or classmates. They sometimes turn their sights on family members. That was the case with 39-year-old security guard, Christopher Speight.

The story began shortly after noon on 19 January 2010 when an injured man was found beside a rural road in Appomattox County, Virginia. He was soaked in blood and lying face down.

'I knew something was really strange,' said Speight's neighbour, 29-year-old Tammy Randolph. She started running to Speight's house to call for help but turned back when she came across a second bloody body in the road.

A deputy who went to investigate fled after he heard gunshots. When the wounded man was finally rescued, he was barely alive and died on the way to hospital.

Four more bodies were found outside a nearby brown colonial-style home. Another three were inside. They were Speight's sister, her family and friends.

The killer was thought to still be alive. A manhunt began as police searched a wood to the west of Appomattox where the suspect was thought to be hiding. A National Guard helicopter flying overhead was struck at least four times. No one was hurt, but a bullet ruptured the fuel tank and the helicopter was forced to land. Dogs and thermal imaging units were brought in, and four local schools were closed. The police surrounded the wood, setting up a perimeter of 18 sq km (7 sq miles), while gunfire was directed at them.

'He was right over that tree line,' said a local. 'That's where he was shooting. He knew what he was doing.'

The following day, after a 20-hour stand-off, Speight gave himself up to the police. He was wearing a bullet-proof vest, but was not carrying the high-powered rifle, which he was thought to have used to fire on the helicopter. He was arrested and charged with first-degree murder and taken to Blue Ridge Regional Jail in Lynchburg.

Gunfire at night

Speight was the co-owner of the house where the bodies were found. He appeared to have booby-trapped the property, but the explosives found inside and around the house were detonated safely by a bomb squad.

Co-workers said that Speight had seemed sullen and on edge when he showed up for work as a security guard at a small grocery store not long before the incident. He had been distant since his mother died of cancer in 2006, they said, but in recent months he had become increasingly angry with family members, who he believed were trying to steal the farmhouse his mother had bequeathed to him and his sister. He feared the family would evict him.

'On Saturday, he was here,' said Tonya Maddox, a cashier at the store, 'and he wouldn't come inside. He wouldn't talk to anybody. We joked that he was going to shoot someone.'

Co-workers also mentioned the fact that Speight was a devout Jehovah's Witness.

Roger Harris, a 36-year-old mechanic and farmer who worked on the property next to Speight's, said he was accustomed to hearing guns. Speight was a gun enthusiast and enjoyed target shooting at the range on his property. But the shooting had recently became a daily occurrence, with Speight firing high-powered rifles.

'Then we noticed he was doing it at night-time,' said a neighbour, and the gunfire began coming from deeper in the woods.

All of the dead were either family members or friends of the family. One of Speight's relatives, who picked up the phone at the home of Speight's

Christopher Speight, perpetrator of the worst mass killing in Virginia since the Virginia Tech massacre.

uncle, Jack Giglio, in Tampa, Florida when reporters called, said she was sickened by the news. She said Speight had last been seen by many members of the family at his mother's funeral.

Possessed by demons

'This is a horrific tragedy,' state police spokeswoman Corinne Geller said. 'It's definitely one of the worst mass killings in Virginia, probably since the Virginia Tech tragedy in April 2007.'

The eight dead were Speight's sister, Lauralee Sipe, 38; her husband, Dwayne S Sipe, also 38; her daughter, Morgan Dobyns, 15; their son, Joshua Sipe, four; their friends, Jonathan Quarles, 43; his wife, Karen Quarles, also 43; their daughter, Emily Quarles, 15; and her boyfriend, Ronald 'Bo' Scruggs, 16.

On 24 June 2010, Appomattox County Circuit Court Judge Richard Blanton signed an order declaring Speight incompetent to stand trial. He was sent to a state psychiatric hospital until such time as he is able to assist his attorneys with his defence.

It seems that the three Sipes in the house were killed two days before Speight fatally shot the other five victims. Investigators said Speight told them that he had been ordered by an Egyptian goddess named Jennifer to shoot his family, because they were possessed by demons. The others were killed, he said, so they could not help his first victims, since Jennifer demanded that their bodies had to rot.

On 15 February 2013, Speight was sentenced in a plea deal to five life terms plus 18 years on three counts of capital murder, one count of attempted capital murder of a police officer and five firearms counts.

Until Speight's killing spree, Appomattox was most famous as the site of the signing of the surrender ending the American Civil War.

CHAPTER 27

Baekuni

1993-2010

On 8 January 2010, a Jakarta street vendor named Baekuni admitted killing 14 street children aged six to 12. He sodomized them either before or after they were dead, and after 2006 he decapitated and mutilated his victims after strangling them with a rope. At first, he simply cut the body in two – later into four – and dumped their bodies.

He was caught when the body parts of nine-year-old Ardiansyah were found in a black plastic bag in a nearby river. According to a psychologist, who interviewed the 48-year-old Baekuni in prison, he was caught because he deviated from his usual procedure of luring victims who were strangers from outside his neighbourhood.

Ardiansyah was a local boy whose mother knew that he was spending a lot of time in Baekuni's home in the months before the murder. She immediately suspected that he was responsible.

Rootless individual

Baekuni was the son of a farmer from Magelang, Central Java. His education did not progress past third grade in primary school. Moving to Jakarta, the capital of Indonesia, he became homeless and began sleeping in Lapangan Banteng park. There, apparently, he began practising sodomy. He moved on to Kunigan, West Java, where he herded buffalo.

At 21, he married, but it seems he could not maintain an erection with a woman. When his wife died, he went back to Jakarta, where he sold cigarettes and cared for street children. They called him 'Badeh', an affectionate term for 'Dad'. He was known for having a soft heart for homeless children, taking many home and giving them temporary shelter 'without molesting them'.

Baekuni, Indonesian child killer.

It seems he knew another child-killer named Siswanto 'Robot' Gedek, who died of a heart attack in 2007 while on death row for raping and killing 12 boys in the mid-1990s. They both worked the same streets, with the homeless Gedek selling plastic bottles for recycling.

It is also thought that he appeared as a witness at Gedek's trial under the name Sunarto. Baekuni changed his name frequently. At any rate, a man thought to be Baekuni testified that he saw Gedek take a little boy into a bush in the former airport area in Kemayoran, Central Jakarta, in 1995.

'The witness saw it from 20 metres away and he only saw movements in the bush,' said lawyer, Febry Irmansyah. 'I'm 100 per cent sure that Sunarto was a dead-ringer for Baekuni.'

'When Baekuni was arrested, he said it was Robot Gedek who did it,' Febry said, though Gedek was dead by them.

Robot Gedek and Baekuni had a similar pattern. They would sodomize their victims before getting rid of their bodies.

'Robot Gedek would take his victims to play video games, feed them and sodomize them, before strangling them with a rope and disposing of their bodies,' Febry said.

Baekuni also used a rope, but he would kill his victims before sodomizing them. Their motive was different. Baekuni said he killed his victims because they refused to be sodomized.

'Robot Gedek killed because he was afraid people would find out that he sodomized children,' Febry said.

Tried and convicted for the sexual abuse and murder of four street children, Baekuni was sentenced to life imprisonment on 5 October 2010.

CHAPTER 28

Derrick Bird

2 June 2010

Nobody knows why mild-mannered taxi driver, Derrick Bird, 52, from the village of Rowrah took off around West Cumbria, killing 12 people and injuring a further 11, before taking his own life. Everyone who knew him said it was out of character, and no one knew he had a gun. He should have been a happy man as he had just become a grandfather, though his mother was terminally ill.

He began by shooting his twin brother, David, in nearby Lamplugh, then the family solicitor, Kevin Commons, 60, in Frizington, 6 km (4 miles) away. The police received a telephone call about the incident at 10.20am. Thirteen minutes later, he shot dead a fellow taxi driver, Darren Rewcastle, 43, at the rank in Whitehaven 8 km (5 miles) farther on, and he fired shots at several others. Meanwhile, residents of Whitehaven and Egremont and Seascale to the south were told to stay indoors, while Bird drove around shooting at random.

Drive-by shootings

On the streets of Egremont, he killed 71-year-old Kenneth Fishburn and 57-year-old Susan Hughes. In the village of Wilton to the east, 67-year-old James Jackson and his 68-year-old wife, Jennifer, were shot dead. The next victim was 65-year-old mole-catcher, Isaac Dixon, in a field outside Carleton.

A former semi-professional rugby league player, Garry Purdham, 31, was shot dead outside the Red Admiral Hotel at Boonhead, near Gosforth. Bird then killed 23-year-old Jamie Clark, 64-year-old Michael Pike and 66-year-old Jane Robinson at Seascale. The gates of the nearby Sellafield nuclear reprocessing plant were closed and the afternoon shift were told not to report for work.

Bird's dark grey Citroën Xsara Picasso was found abandoned in the remote village of Boot, 16 km (10 miles) inland. At 2pm, Bird's body was found alongside a gun in a wooded area nearby. He had had a shotgun licence since 1995 and a licence for a rifle since then.

CHAPTER 29

Elias Abuelazam

2 August 2010

Israeli immigrant Elias Abuelazam was suspected of 18 random stabbings, five of which were fatal, but he was only convicted of one – that of 49-year-old Arnold Minor on 2 August 2010. But as he was sentenced to life in prison without the possibility of parole, the other cases were dropped. The attacks largely took place in and around Flint, Michigan, and the victims by and large were Black, so it was thought that there could have been a racial motivation behind them.

Abuelazam was born in 1976 to a middle-class Christian-Arab family in the city of Ramla, central Israel. He moved to the US in the 1990s and obtained a green card as a permanent resident. Two marriages ended in divorce. His brushes with the law started in 1995, when he was charged with fraud in California. In 2008, he served about a month in jail in Virginia for not disclosing this on an application for a handgun permit. Until then, he worked at Piedmont Behavioral Health Center, a psychiatric facility in Leesburg, Virginia, as a mental health technician.

Colleagues there could not believe it when they heard about the stabbings.

'I just can't see him doing this,' said Paul Lozinsky. 'I can't believe he's the type of guy who would do this. He was a nice guy to me. We got along together.'

'Wow. Maybe a lot has changed,' said his brother, Daniel Lozinsky, who testified at Abuelazam's first divorce proceedings. 'I really didn't know that side of him. He seemed like a caring guy to me.'

Both said that, while Abuelazam was friendly, they did not socialize with him outside work and did not keep in touch once he had moved to Michigan, where he worked in a liquor store in Beecher on the outskirts of Flint. On 29 July 2010, he was cited for giving alcohol to a minor, the same day that there were two stabbings in Flint, one of which Abuelazam was charged with. But at the liquor store, neither patrons nor colleagues found anything unusual about the man they called Eli.

The first stabbing

However, the stabbings may have started in Ramla. Visiting there early in 2010, he was suspected of stabbing a friend in the face with a screwdriver, but the case was dropped when the friend refused to press charges.

The stabbings in Flint began on 24 May 2010, when 31-year-old David Motley was found dead at around 6am. All the stabbings Abuelazam was accused of occurred late at night or in the early hours. However, he was not charged with Motley's slaying.

Nor was he charged with the murder of 59-year-old Emmanuel Abdul Muhammad, who was found dead in Flint at 2am on 21 June. However, he was charged with assault with intent to murder for an attack on 42-year-old Bill Fisher at 5.50am in Clio, Michigan, 10 km (6 miles) to the north.

Abuelazam was also charged with assault with intent to murder for the attack on 29-year-old Antoine Jackson at 1.30am on 12 July in nearby Burton. And again for the attack on Richard Booker at 12.15am on 19 July in Genesee Township to the north.

He was not charged with the stabbing of a 21-year-old man in Flint at 5.45am on 23 July, though he was charged with the murder of 43-year-old Darwin Marshall, who was found stabbed to death at 1.25am on 26 July. The prosecution did not proceed.

The following day, at about 3am, Antwoine Marshall was attacked and Abuelazam was charged with assault with intent to murder. He faced the same charge for the stabbing of 20-year-old Davon Rawls at 3.30am on 29 July, though not for the stabbing of a 59-year-old man nearby at 6am.

The next day, 60-year-old Frank Kellybrew was stabbed to death in Flint Township at around 3.30am and Abuelazam was charged with murder.

But he was not charged with the stabbing of a 28-year-old man at 6am that same day.

Abuelazam was charged with assault with intent to murder for the attack on 18-year-old Etwan Wilson at 2.30am on 1 August. The following day came the attack on Arnold Minor, whose murder Abuelazam was convicted of.

He was not charged in connection with the attack on 15-year-old Anthony Kage out jogging at night on 3 August in Leesburg, Virginia, who was stabbed in the back by an assailant who did not say a word. At around 1.15am on 5 August, Abuelazam was stopped by the police in nearby Arlington County on an outstanding minor assault warrant from Leesburg that had nothing to do with the stabbings, though it was noted that he had a knife and a hammer in his SUV. He appeared before a magistrate and was released on his own recognizance. Then, just after 6am, a 67-year-old man sitting on his apartment stoop in Leesburg was approached by a man who stabbed him in the back without saying a word. Again, Abuelazam faced no charge.

The next day, a 19-year-old man was asked for assistance in fixing a dark green Chevrolet Blazer SUV in a Leesburg parking lot when he was hit on the head with a hammer. Once again, Abuelazam was not charged.

Finally, Abuelazam was indicted for the stabbing of a 59-year-old man outside a church in Toledo, Ohio, on 7 August. Sixteen of the men he attacked were Black, one a dark-skinned Hispanic and one white. Survivors said that he often asked for directions or assistance before attacking them.

Running out of time

However, the hammer attack in the Leesburg parking lot had been caught on CCTV. Leesburg detectives noticed similarities to the Michigan cases and the authorities put out a public plea for help in finding the Blazer.

An anonymous tip led the police to the liquor store where Abuelazam worked. Co-workers told police he hadn't been at work for a while because

Elias Abuelazam thought 'evil forces' were controlling him.

he was visiting family in Virginia. Other survivors said they had seen the SUV and a friend of Darwin Marshall had also seen Abuelazam's Blazer, when she witnessed Marshall's murder.

The Blazer was found behind Abuelazam's uncle's house in Flint, where he had been living. Meanwhile, airline records revealed that he had boarded a plane from Detroit to Louisville, Kentucky, then flown on to Atlanta. He was paged over the loudspeakers at Hartsfield-Jackson Atlanta International Airport, where he was about to board Delta Flight 152 for Tel Aviv, and arrested by US Customs and Border Protection agents.

'When we finally caught him, there was a cheer that erupted,' said Genesee County Prosecutor, David Leyton, who was waiting for word of the capture at the state police post in Flint Township, where the task force was headquartered. 'It was very exciting.'

Abuelazam waived his rights and was extradited back to Michigan where he was held in solitary confinement in Genesee County Jail. There, a man tried to poison him and he attacked a prison guard.

'The longer he is locked up, the more of a problem he is becoming,' Sheriff Robert Pickell said. 'He is more demanding, thinking the sheriff's trying to poison him.'

Arnold Minor's blood was found on a pair of jeans and trainers in his luggage and on the steering wheel and floor of his SUV. Abuelazam's defence pleaded that he was not guilty by reason of insanity. A psychiatrist testified that he was a paranoid schizophrenic who believed that 'evil forces' were controlling his actions. Expert witnesses for the prosecution rebutted this. Abuelazam was convicted and sentenced to spend the rest of his life in jail.

CHAPTER 30

Nordine Amrani

13 December 2011

Expectant shoppers were waiting for the opening of the Christmas Fair in Place Saint-Lambert, a square in the centre of Liège, when grenades rained down on them and rifle fire rent the air. Within minutes, six were dead and 125 others injured.

The perpetrator was 33-year-old Nordine Amrani, a Belgian of Moroccan origin and a welder by trade. He had been orphaned at an early age and had grown up in foster homes.

'I remember a man deeply marked by the loss of his parents,' said his family lawyer, Abdelhadi Amrani, no relation. 'He lost his father and mother very early. He was marked by fate. I would add he was a very smart boy, gifted. Nordine often spoke of his desire to start a family. He was to be married in Liège to a nurse.'

His girlfriend dismissed any possible terrorist motives for the attack.

'He did not feel at all Moroccan. He did not speak a word of Arabic and was not Muslim. What he said is that he felt a Belgian,' she said. 'He was crazy about weapons, but as a collector. He felt he had not had much luck in life and felt unfairly treated by the courts. This was a "*ras-le-bol*" [expression of discontent] of a tormented soul: estranged from justice, and against society.'

He was constantly in trouble with the law, according to Liège chief prosecutor, Cedric Visart de Bocarme.

'He was a felon who had been in trouble all his life: youth court, criminal court, courts of appeal,' he said.

He had, among other things, a vice conviction in 2003, along with one for handling stolen goods and conspiracy.

Gun freak

A weapons aficionado, he was said to be able to dismantle, repair and put together all sorts of weapons but he was never linked to any terrorist act or network, AFP news agency reported.

When he was arrested in 2008, police found 2,800 cannabis plants he was growing in a warehouse. They also found ten guns and 9,500 rounds of ammunition. The arsenal included a Law rocket launcher, an AK-47 assault rifle, a sniper rifle, a K31 rifle, a Fal assault rifle and hundreds of cartridges.

'Amrani made silencers himself,' the newspaper *Le Soir* said. 'At the time, Amrani refused to say where the weapons had come from and where they were destined.'

He was sentenced to five years, but on appeal the gun conviction was overturned due to 'grey areas' left by a change in classification in Belgium's gun laws of June 2006. He was released in October 2010 and was living with his fiancée in a 1930s apartment building, the Residence Belvedere, a five-minute drive from Saint-Lambert Square.

Under pressure

On the day of the attack, he was due to report to a Liège police station at 1.30pm to answer allegations that he had sexually molested a young woman. He was said to have attacked the unnamed victim after driving alongside her in his van, whose registration number was picked out by CCTV.

'He was afraid of being sent back to prison,' said Jean-François Dister, a criminal defence lawyer handling the case. 'He phoned me twice – on Monday afternoon and on Tuesday morning.'

One of Amrani's numerous previous convictions was for rape; he had been given a two-year suspended sentence in 2003. If convicted again for a sex crime, he would have had to serve time. This would have also meant his fiancée, a nurse called Perrin Balon, who worked for a home-care company, would find out about the sex allegations against him.

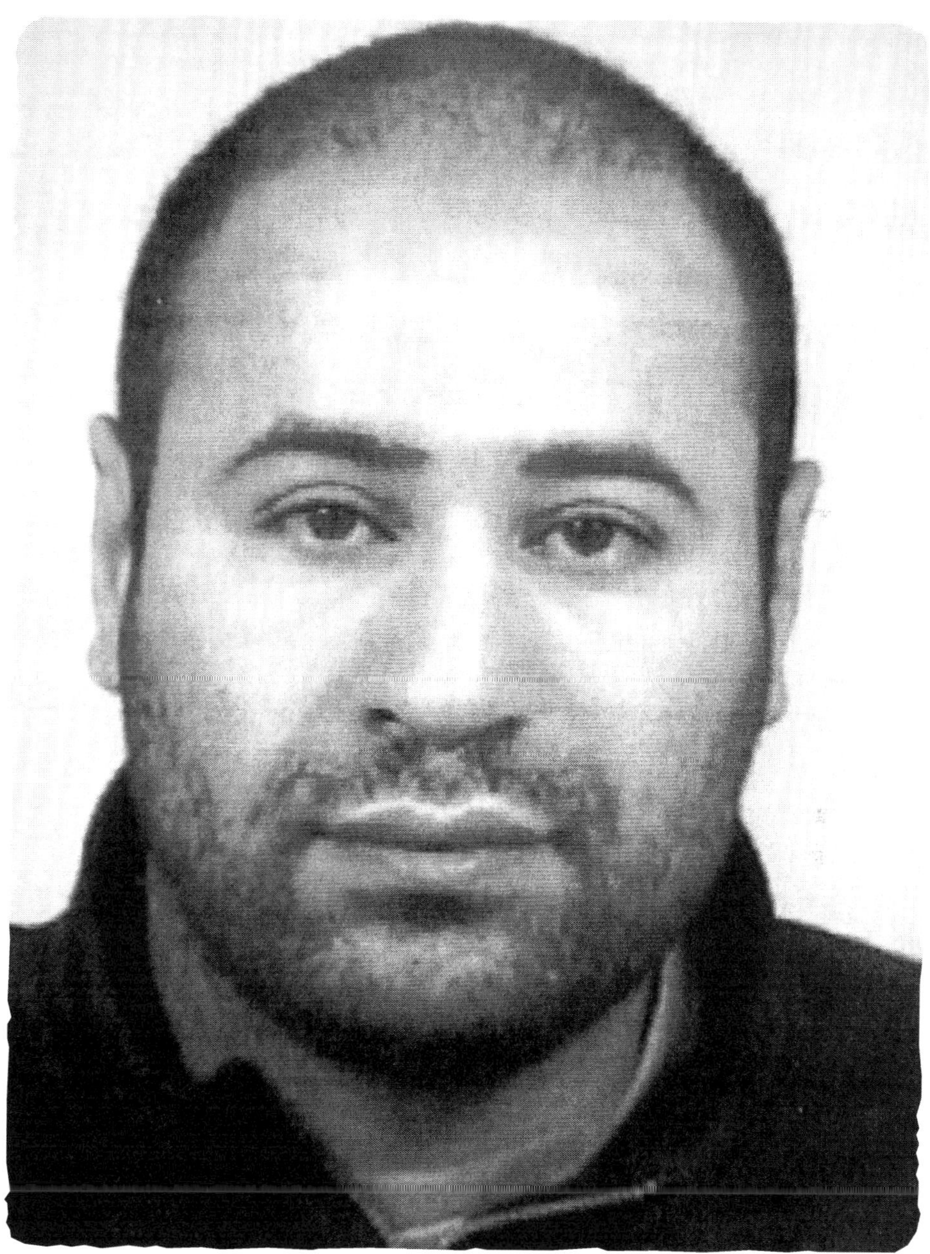

Nordine Amrani killed at a Christmas Fair in Liège, Belgium.

'It seemed the new case was not particularly serious, but Mr Amrani thought he was being picked on,' the lawyer said. 'He explained to me that he had been questioned over an abduction. According to him, he had been framed and someone was out to get him. Mr Amrani had a grudge against the law. He thought he had been wrongfully convicted.'

That morning, it appeared that Amrani had lured a neighbour's cleaning woman into his flat and attacked her.

'The cleaner had been working in a neighbour's home,' said the police. 'It appears that Amrani had invited her into his own flat to discuss the possibility of cleaning his flat. There were signs of a struggle, and it may be that Amrani had tried to rape her. Whatever happened, she was undoubtedly his first murder victim on Tuesday morning.'

He had put a bullet in her head and dumped her body in a lock-up where he was growing more cannabis. Then, he transferred money into Ms Balon's account with a note saying: 'Good luck! I love you.'

Carrying a Belgian-made FN-FAL automatic rifle, a handgun and up to a dozen grenades in a backpack, he drove to Place Saint-Lambert. After parking his van, he walked on to a raised walkway above a bakery overlooking lunchtime shoppers, who were getting ready for the opening of the Christmas market. From his vantage point 4.5 m (15 ft) above the ground, he lobbed three hand grenades towards a busy bus shelter in the city-centre square before opening fire on the crowd.

Victims included two teenage boys, aged 15 and 17, a 17-month-old baby and a 75-year-old woman. Then he turned a .367 Magnum on himself. His bag still contained a number of loaded magazines and several live grenades.

CHAPTER 31

Israel Keyes

2011–2012

Israel Keyes was a dedicated serial killer. He studied the subject. Dozens of books about murder were found in his home. As a youth, he had read *Mindhunter: Inside the FBI's Elite Serial Crime Unit* by FBI profiler John E Douglas.

Asked about Robert Hansen who kidnapped, raped and murdered at least 17 women in Alaska between 1972 and 1983, he said: 'Yeah, I know all about him. I probably know every single serial killer that's ever been written about. It's kind of a hobby of mine.'

Dennis Rader – the BTK (bind, torture, kill) killer who murdered at least ten people in Kansas over a 30-year career – was 'a wimp', he said, for apologizing for his crimes. His heroes were serial killers who had not been caught yet.

Ted Bundy, who raped and murdered dozens of young women in the 1970s, was a particular favourite. But they were very different.

'If you recall Ted Bundy, he was kind of the opposite; he revelled in attention,' said Anchorage homicide detective Monique Doll, who worked on the Keyes case. 'Israel Keyes was the exact opposite in that way. He very deliberately did not want to be titled a "serial killer" because it would draw attention to him, and it would draw the media down on his loved ones. He was very protective of his friends and family.'

Confessing to as many as 12 murders, Israel Keyes was asked why he did it. He replied. 'Why not?'

His motivation was enjoyment, said Detective Doll.

'Israel Keyes didn't kidnap and kill people because he was crazy,' she told a news conference. 'He didn't kidnap and kill people because his deity told him to or because he had a bad childhood. Israel Keyes did this because he got an immense amount of enjoyment out of it, much like an addict gets an immense amount of enjoyment out of drugs.'

He also enjoyed staying under the radar, officials said. Emulating Bundy, he targeted total strangers, avoiding anyone he had any possible connection to, travelling hundreds of kilometres to murder random victims in secluded parks and other remote locations. But then he got caught because he broke all his own rules.

Losing his religion

Born in 1978, Israel Keyes grew up in Washington State in a fundamentalist Christian family that attended a white-supremacist, anti-semitic church. Later, they moved out of the region and became affiliated with other congregations.

His parents threw him out when he admitted being an atheist. He then developed an interest in Satanism.

Keyes admitted to torturing animals as a child and raping a teenager in Oregon in the late-1990s. He managed to lure the girl, aged between 14 and 18, away from her friends, stripped her and tied her up. He had intended to kill her in a Satanic ritual, but in the end let her go when she wouldn't stop talking.

'I was too timid. I wasn't violent enough,' he said later. 'I made up my mind I was never going to let that happen again.'

Keyes served in the US Army from 1998 through 2000. Stationed in Egypt, he travelled to Tel Aviv to sleep with prostitutes. He also admitted two rapes. Meanwhile, he fantasized about killing strangers.

'I guess you could say I came to terms with myself and the reasons I wanted to do it,' he said.

He quit the Army, so that he could travel freely and commit murder. He worked as a handyman, paying for his travel with burglary and by robbing banks. In 2007, he moved to Anchorage, Alaska, with his Native American girlfriend and their daughter. There, he set up a construction business. But the desire to murder was too much for him.

He kept what he called 'murder kits' near his home in Anchorage and in New York state, where he had a run-down cabin on 4 hectares (10 acres) of land. The one found in Alaska included a shovel, plastic bags and bottles of Drano, which he told authorities would speed up the decomposition of bodies. The murder kit found in upstate New York contained weapon parts, a silencer, ligatures, ammunition and garbage bags. Keyes said other murder kits were hidden in Washington State, Wyoming, Texas and somewhere in the Southwest, possibly Arizona. There was also one in Vermont, which he had hidden there two years before he committed a double murder nearby.

Fatal mistakes

Despite this meticulous planning, on the spur of the moment, on 1 February 2012, he kidnapped 18-year-old barista Samantha Koenig in Anchorage. CCTV footage showed him approaching her kiosk as she was closing up at around 8pm and ordering an Americano. While she was making it, he pulled a gun. He climbed into the kiosk and bound her hands behind her back with zip ties, before leading her out. She had not pushed the panic button because he told her that he would let her go if her parents paid a ransom. That was never his intention.

The FBI said Koenig broke away at some point and Keyes chased her, tackling her to bring her to the ground. Pointing his gun at her, he said she should not do anything to make him kill her. More video footage showed him forcing her into the back of his 2004 Chevrolet Silverado in the parking lot of Home Depot. The police drew up a list of 750 white trucks of the same make in the area, but the licence plate, toolboxes and a ladder rack he usually carried had been removed before the abduction. They were reinstalled afterwards, effectively disguising the vehicle.

Samantha was sexually assaulted and strangled. Her body was left in a cold shed for two weeks, while her killer went on a cruise. When he returned, he posed her body to make it look like she was still alive, alongside a newspaper dated 13 February, 12 days after the abduction. On the back of the photograph, he wrote a ransom note demanding $30,000 from her family. He then sent a text to her boyfriend from her cell phone, telling him where to find the note in a nearby dog park. At other times, the batteries were removed from the cell phone, so it could not be traced. He dismembered her body and dropped it in a frozen lake north of Anchorage, after cutting a hole through the ice with a chainsaw.

The next mistake he made was using her debit card on a trip to the southwestern US. His rental car was caught on video when he was using it at

Israel Keyes studied how to be a serial killer.

an ATM in Texas. Then, he was stopped for speeding, but federal agents were already on his trail and he was arrested.

Extradited back to Alaska, he admitted a series of burglaries, bank robberies and murders, though fell silent when his name was leaked to the press. The authorities had difficulty identifying the murder victims as Keyes rarely knew their names. However, the victims of a double murder in Vermont were identified as William and Lorraine Currier, a middle-aged couple who lived in Essex, Vermont. He flew from Anchorage to Chicago and then drove 1,600 km (1,000 miles) to their home. He chose it because it had an attached garage. There was no evidence of children or a dog, and he was familiar with that style of house and knew where the master bedroom was.

He broke into their bedroom, bound the couple with zip ties, forced them into their car and drove them to an abandoned farmhouse. There, he shot William, and sexually assaulted and strangled Lorraine. The house has since been torn down and their bodies couldn't be found. However, Samantha Koenig's body parts were recovered.

In the annals of serial killers, Keyes is a rare bird. He was never convicted of murder and administered his own capital punishment. While in jail awaiting trial, he slit his wrist and strangled himself with a bedsheet. He left a suicide note. On it, there were drawings of 11 skulls and a pentagram with the head of the Satanic goat, Baphomet, in it.

With no one to try, the case had to be dropped.

'It gives us no pleasure to dismiss the charges against Mr Keyes, but that's what the law requires,' said Kevin Feldis, the assistant US attorney leading the prosecution.

CHAPTER 32

Robert Bales

11 March 2012

Post Traumatic Stress Disorder can lead to psychosis. That may have been proved by 38-year-old US Army Sergeant Robert Bales, a decorated veteran of three tours of duty in Iraq, who shot and stabbed nine children, four men and three women in the village of Alkozai in Kandahar Province, Afghanistan.

But then Bales had already been in trouble. In 2001, he had been found liable for financial fraud related to the handling of a retirement account and ordered to pay $1.4 million in civil damages. He never paid a penny. The financial services company he had co-founded went out of business and he enlisted.

Bales was initially assigned to the 2nd Battalion, 3rd Infantry of the 3rd Stryker Brigade, 2nd Infantry Division in Fort Lewis. He completed three tours in the Iraq War: 12 months in 2003 and 2004, 15 months in 2006 and 2007, and ten months in 2009 and 2010.

He was described by one former platoon leader as 'one of the best soldiers I ever worked with', and a man who prided himself on identifying 'the bad guys from non-combatants'.

In the 2007 tour, he reportedly injured his foot in the Battle of Najaf, and in the 2010 tour he was treated in Fort Lewis for traumatic brain injury after his vehicle was rolled in an accident, but he was deemed healthy.

Living on the edge

Meanwhile, things were not going smoothly off the battlefield. In 2002, he got into a fight with a security guard at a Tacoma area casino and was charged with a misdemeanour criminal assault, but the charge was dismissed after he paid a small fine and attended anger management classes. Another confrontation outside a bar in 2008 was also reported to police, but no charges were filed. That same year, he was arrested after he drove his car off a road and into a tree, then fled the scene. Witnesses told police that he was bleeding, disoriented and smelled of alcohol, but he was not charged with drunk driving.

There were also troubles at home. His wife, Karilyn, was struggling with the finances needed to bring up their infant sons in Washington state. They had fallen behind on mortgage payments and put their home up for sale, but the property was listed for $50,000 less than what they paid for it in 2005, and less than they owed the bank. Bales was also disappointed after being passed over for promotion, though Karilyn saw at least one reason for optimism. They understood he had served his final tour in a war zone, and that they and their two young children would soon move to a non-combat posting. Her husband was, after all, a loving father and husband and the 'life and soul of the party'.

On 1 February 2012, Bales was assigned to Camp Belambay in Kandahar Province, where he was responsible for providing base security for US Army Special Forces and US Navy SEALs who were engaged in village stability operations.

A bomb had gone off on 8 March, destroying an armoured vehicle and wounding several US soldiers. Villagers said that afterwards US soldiers lined many of the male villagers against a wall, threatening to 'get revenge for this incident by killing at least 20 of your people', and threatening that 'you and your children will pay for this'. Then, Bales had seen a fellow soldier have his leg blown off in an explosion.

Hellbent on trouble

On 11 March 2012, after a night of drinking contraband alcohol, snorting Valium and watching movies with other soldiers, Sergeant Bales slipped away from his combat outpost and set off toward the villages. He was wearing night-vision googles and traditional Afghan clothing over his fatigues.

'I left the VSP [Village Stability Platform] and went to the nearby village of Alkozai,' Bales told the judge, Colonel Jeffery Nance. 'While inside a compound in Alkozai, I observed a female I now know to be Na'ikmarga. I formed the intent to kill Na'ikmarga, and I did kill Na'ikmarga by shooting her with a firearm. This act was without legal justification, sir.'

'Did you go there expecting to find them there?' asked Nance.

'Sir, I expected someone to be there,' Bales said, adding, 'Sir, I intended to kill them.'

Bales returned to his base between attacking the villages, woke up a fellow soldier and confessed. The soldier didn't believe him and went back to sleep, and Bales left again to continue the slaughter.

Most of the victims were women and children, and some of the bodies were piled up and burned. The slayings drew such angry protests that the US temporarily halted combat operations in Afghanistan. It was three weeks before American investigators could reach the crime scenes.

Four members of the same family were killed in Alkozai. According to a 16-year-old boy who was shot in the leg, the soldier woke up his family members before shooting them. Another witness said she saw the man drag a woman out of her house and repeatedly hit her head against a wall.

The first victim in Najiban appears to have been Mohammad Dawoud. According to Dawoud's brother, the assailant shot Dawoud in the head but spared his wife and six children after the wife screamed at him.

Eleven members of Abdul Samad's family were killed, including his wife, four girls between the ages of two and six, four boys between eight and 12, and two other relatives. According to a witness, 'he dragged the boys by their hair and shot them in the mouth'. At least three of the child victims were killed by a single shot to the head. Witnesses reported that the perpetrator was wearing a headlamp and/or a spotlight attached to his weapon.

The perpetrator burned some of the victims' bodies, an act that would be considered desecration under Islamic law. Witnesses said that the 11 corpses from one family were shot in the head, stabbed, and then gathered together in one room and set on fire. A pile of ashes was found on the floor of one victim's house; at least one child's body was found partially charred.

Afghan forces spotted Bales leaving. A head count back at the US base confirmed that a man was missing, but Bales returned and gave himself up before a search party could be organized.

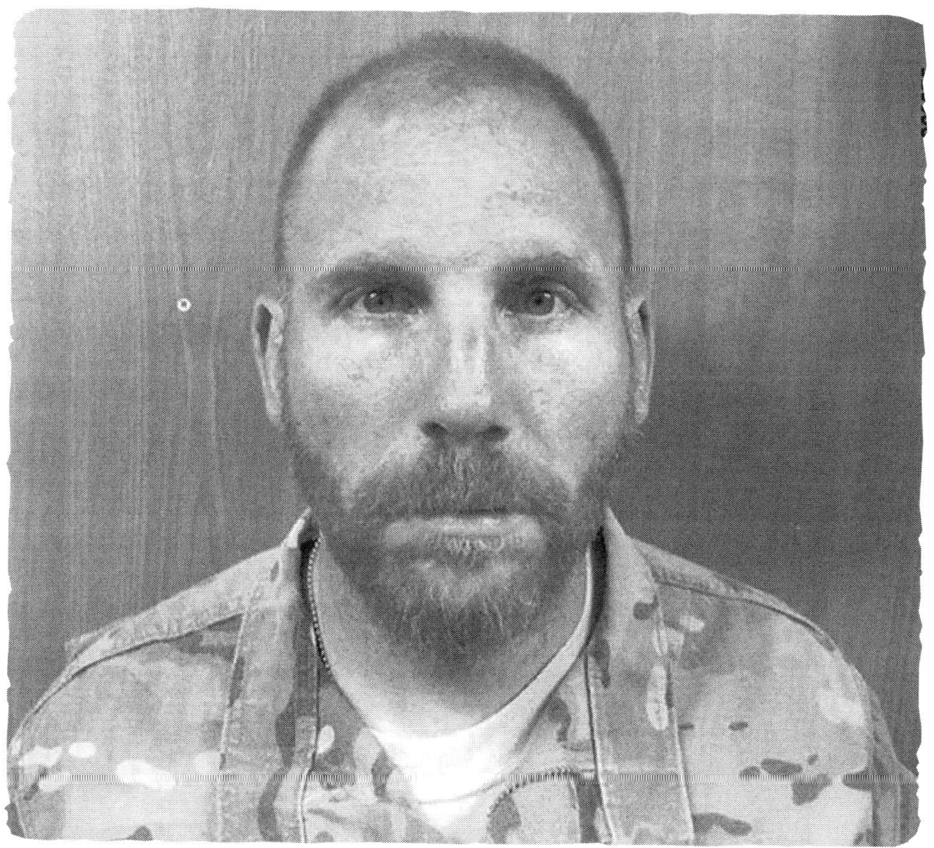

Robert Bales admitted killing for no good reason.

Coming clean

Bales was flown out to Kuwait, then on to Fort Leavenworth, Kansas. He was charged with 16 counts of murder, six counts of attempted murder and seven counts of assault, along with abuse of steroids, alcohol consumption in a combat zone and attempting to destroy evidence.

In a plea bargain to avoid the death penalty, he pleaded guilty on all charges.

'What was your reason for killing them?' Colonel Nance asked.

Bales said he had asked himself that question 'a million times' and added: 'There's not a good reason in this world for why I did the horrible things I did.'

Asked by Colonel Nance whether he had poured kerosene on some of his victims and set them on fire as the charges against him specified, Sergeant Bales said he remembered seeing a kerosene lamp in one of the village compounds, and later found matches in his pocket. But did the bodies set themselves on fire, he was asked. He did not remember what happened, he said. Then, he conceded that the cumulative evidence was clear that it must have happened, and that he must, in fact, have done it.

'It's the only thing that makes sense, sir,' Bales said.

He said he took steroids illegally because he had wanted to get stronger, or 'huge and jacked'. Asked by the judge what other effects the drugs might have had, Bales said: 'Sir, it definitely increased my irritability and anger.'

He was sentenced to life in prison without parole. He was also demoted to the lowest enlisted rank, dishonourably discharged and made to forfeit all pay and allowances.

Afghan survivors were outraged that he was not sentenced to death.

Mohammed Wazir, who had 11 family members killed that night, including his mother and two-year-old daughter, said: 'Hang him. That's what I want. Hang him from the neck; let him dangle… If your child dies, what would you expect? Money? No.' Wazir denied taking the compensation that the US government offered to the victims of the massacre. 'Will you expect prison? We don't want prison… If the court doesn't go the way we want, we will not accept the decision of the court.'

He vowed: 'For this one thing, we would kill 100 American soldiers.'

The New York Times called the massacre at Kandahar 'the worst American war crime in recent memory'. The atrocity brought US-Afghan relations to a new low, prompting 'Death to America' protests in Afghanistan, and fresh calls for the timetable for the 2014 withdrawal of American and British forces to be accelerated.

CHAPTER 33

Mikhail Popkov

23 June 2012

While the murders Mikhail Viktorovich Popkov was convicted of were committed between 1992 and 2010, Russian authorities are convinced that the deaths continued up until the time of his arrest on 23 June 2012. Indeed, he admitted as much.

Mikhail Popkov was known as The Werewolf in the press because he struck at night and he was, perhaps, Russia's most prolific serial killer. He admitted to the rape and murder of more than 80 women, though there may have been many more.

After he had been sentenced to life imprisonment for 22 murders in 2015, Popkov claimed to have stopped killing in the year 2000, when one of his victims gave him syphilis and rendered him impotent. Then, in 2017, he admitted that he continued killing for another ten years and confessed to the murder of another 60 women in the Irkutsk oblast of central Siberia.

Popkov had been a police officer. But after quitting the force, he travelled regularly between his hometown of Angarsk and Vladivostok on Russia's Pacific coast, over 3,200 km (2,000 miles) away, and homicide officers feel that he may have killed many victims along the way. They believed that he was gradually doling out his confessions to delay his transfer from the relative comfort of a regular prison to the tough, inhospitable penal colony where he was destined to serve out the rest of his life sentence.

Wife's affair

Popkov began killing in 1992 when he found two used condoms in the trash at his home and suspected that his wife Elena, who was also a police officer, was cheating on him. Although it seems likely that the condoms had actually been left by a house guest, one of Elena's work colleagues later admitted that he had a brief affair with her.

A few weeks after his discovery, Popkov 'spontaneously' discovered the need to kill, as he told investigators.

'I just felt I wanted to kill a woman I was giving a lift to in my car,' he said.

In 2015, he had claimed his aim was to 'cleanse' his hometown of prostitution. Even if his victims were not prostitutes, he felt that women who went out by themselves at night to drink alcohol in bars should be punished. The theory was that Popkov was taking some sort of psychic revenge on an alcoholic mother who abused him as a child.

'My victims were women who walked the streets at night alone, without men, and not sober, who behaved thoughtlessly, carelessly and were not afraid to engage in a conversation with me, sit in the car, and then go for a drive in search of adventure, for the sake of entertainment, ready to drink alcohol and have sexual intercourse with me,' he said.

The women were reassured by his police uniform and felt safe getting into a police car late at night.

'I was in uniform. I decided to stop and give a woman a ride, I frequently did that before,' he said.

After he'd had sex with them, he decided whether to murder them.

'In this way, not all women became victims, but women of certain negative behaviour, and I had a desire to teach and punish them,' he said. 'So that others would not behave in such a way, and so that they would be afraid.'

The process was simple.

'The woman began talking to me, I offered to give her a lift, she agreed... That same morning, I drove the head of the criminal investigation to the murder scene.'

Not only did Popkov get a thrill from killing his victims, he also went on to have sex with their dead bodies afterwards. Then, he multiplied his pleasure by reliving every detail of the crime by getting involved in the investigation as a serving officer.

Close shave

He was lucky not to have been caught early on in his career as one of his victims survived and identified him. On 26 January 1998, a 15-year-old known as Svetlana M said a police car had stopped and offered her a lift. The officer took her into woodland where he forced her to strip naked. He then smashed her head against a tree. She lost consciousness.

He left her for dead, but the next day she was found alive near the village of Baykalsk, some 113 km (70 miles) from where she had been picked up. Somehow, she survived the night in the sub-zero temperatures of a Siberian winter without any clothing. When she awoke in hospital, she identified the attacker as a policeman and gave details of his car. However, Popkov's wife provided him with a false alibi. Neither his wife nor their daughter could believe that he was a killer, saying he was a perfect husband and father.

'I had a double life,' he said. 'In one life, I was an ordinary person… In my other life, I committed murders, which I carefully concealed from everyone, realizing that what I was doing was a criminal offence.'

His colleagues in the police force also found it hard to believe that Popkov was a killer. He never seemed to show any signs of mental instability.

'I was in the service, in the police, having positive feedback on my work,' he said. 'I never thought of myself as mentally unhealthy. During my police service, I regularly passed medical commissions and was recognized as fit.'

Risk-taker

But another clue had been overlooked. Some of the murder weapons were taken from the store of those confiscated by the police. After a murder, Popkov would wipe off his fingerprints, then throw the weapon away near the crime scene. Otherwise, he would use anything that came to hand.

'The choice of weapons for killing was always casual,' he said. 'I never prepared beforehand to commit a murder, I could use any object that was in the car – a knife, an axe, a bat.'

Mikhail Popkov – aka The Werewolf – one of Russia's most prolific serial killers.

Nevertheless, he could be fastidious.

'I never used rope for strangulation,' he said, 'and I did not have a firearm either. I did not cut out the hearts of the victims.'

This was not true. He gouged the heart from one victim's body. Others were mutilated or dismembered. A young medical student was beheaded. Her body was found in a rubbish container in Angarsk, her head dumped elsewhere.

And he took chances. One of his victims was a teacher at his own daughter's music school.

'Her corpse was found in the forest along with the body of another woman,' he said. 'My daughter asked me to give her money because the school was collecting to organize funerals. I gave it to her.'

Another close call came in 2000 when he returned to the scene of a double murder. After he had left 35-year-old Maria Lyzhina and 37-year-old

Liliya Pashkovskaya for dead, he found that the chain he wore round his neck was missing and went back to retrieve it.

'I realized that I lost it in a forest glade when I killed two women,' he said. 'I realized that I would absolutely be identified by the lost chain and experienced the greatest stress. I realized that I should return to the scene of the crime, hoping that the police or the prosecutor's office had not been there yet.'

When he returned to the scene, he found the chain right away but spotted that one of the women was still breathing.

'I was shocked by the fact that she was still alive, so I finished off her with a shovel,' he said.

The two women had worked together in a shop. On 2 June, they went to see Maria's sister. At midnight, they headed home. It was a warm summer night, so instead of taking a taxi, they decided to walk. Three days later, their bodies were found in the forest near Veresovka village. Popkov had left their children motherless. Maria had a 14-year-old daughter, Liliya a 12-year-old daughter and three-year-old son.

While it is the customary in Russia for coffins to be left open, the two women's coffins were closed because they were so badly disfigured.

Reported missing

Popkov committed another double murder in 1998. The bodies of 20-year-old Tatiana 'Tanya' Martynova and 19-year-old Yulia Kuprikova were found in a suburb of Angarsk. Tanya's sister, Viktoria Chagaeva, had given her a ticket for a concert. Tanya was married with a small child and her 24-year-old husband, Igor, begged her not to go as there was a killer on the prowl. Ignoring his pleas, she made the mistake of stopping for a quick drink with friends after the show. Then, the two girls accepted a lift from a policeman.

'On the morning of 29 October, Igor called me, saying Tanya had not come back home,' said Viktoria. 'I got truly scared. It was the first time she had ever done this. There were no mobile phones at that time; we could only call Yulia's parents, thinking Tanya must have stayed overnight with them. But Yulia's parents said she had not come home either.'

They went to the police, but were told that they must wait three days before the two young women could be reported missing.

'It was 1am when Tanya's husband Igor and I went to the police,' said Viktoria. 'We did not tell our mother yet. Igor was absolutely devastated and only repeated: "She was killed, she was killed." I was shocked too, but I simply could not believe it and replied: "What are you talking about?"'

That night, a shepherd found their naked bodies near Meget, a village close to Angarsk. Both had been raped after they were dead, then mutilated.

'My elder brother, Oleg, went to the morgue to identify Tanya,' said Viktoria. 'He had just flown in from Moscow. He felt sick when he saw the body, she was so mutilated. He was almost green when he came out of there. He just could not say a word. I did not dare to go in and look.'

Tanya's injuries were to her body and the back of the head, so the coffin could be left open, with her face showing. However, Yulia's coffin had to be closed because her features were so badly mutilated.

'Many people attended Tanya's funeral,' said Viktoria. 'It felt as if the whole town was there. Our poor mother lost consciousness several times; she needed a lot of medicine to cope. Igor was in almost the same condition.'

Indeed, their mother never recovered from the loss of her daughter.

'She felt as if she had died with Tanya, life became useless for her,' said Viktoria. 'She lived only because she was visiting various mediums one by one, looking for the killer and wasting her money. Nobody gave her any serious information, but she kept doing it. She died in 2007, aged 66, from a heart attack. I think her heart could not cope with the pain any longer.'

'An absolutely normal man'

When Popkov was arrested in 2012, Viktoria realized that she knew him. They had both competed in a biathlon at a local sports ground.

'I was stuck with horror when I saw the picture of this maniac in the paper and online,' she said. 'My sister's killer was looking into my eyes. I immediately felt as if I'd met him. Looking at him, I could hardly breathe. Some minutes later, I looked at him another time and thought – oh my God, I know him!'

She was so shocked that she picked up a knife and stabbed the picture of his face in the newspaper.

'I remember him as a tall slim man, he was always alone, with a slippery and shifty gaze,' she said. 'I think such people just must not live. This beast took the life of my sister, who had so many happy years in front of her. I cried a lot that day, but it is time to be quiet and just wait. He will be punished by law and the criminals in jail will punish him, too. I am sure he will pay for all the murders one day.'

That a fellow officer committed these terrible crimes under their noses perturbed the police. A former police colleague said: 'When I read about him in the press, I literally choked because I used to work with him and thought I knew him. He was an absolutely normal man. He liked biathlon; once on duty, he shot a rapist during an arrest. There was an investigation and he was not punished. The chiefs considered he had behaved properly.'

Another ex-colleague said: 'I worked closely with him for five years. He knew lots of jokes and stories, and could be the life and soul of the party.'

Popkov was caught when 3,500 policemen and former policemen were asked to provide a DNA sample. His matched that in sperm found on some of the victims.

'I couldn't have predicted DNA tests,' he told a reporter from *Komsomolskaya Pravda* in a jailhouse interview. 'I was born in the wrong century.'

When Popkov pleaded guilty to 22 murders and two attempted murders in 2015, the judge asked him how many murders he had committed in total. In reply, the killer just shrugged.

'I can't say exactly,' he said. 'I didn't write them down.'

Two years later, he confessed to a further 59 murders. He was convicted of 56; the other three could not be confirmed due to lack of evidence. He was sentenced to a second term of life. Two years after that, he admitted to a further two murders and begged for the death penalty. But capital punishment was still suspended. Detectives believe that he could have killed as many as 200.

CHAPTER 34

Melanie Jane Smith

19 October 2012

Lee-Anna Shiers, 20, her four-year-old nephew, Bailey, and two-year-old niece, Skye, were trapped in their upstairs flat and died in an arson attack in Prestatyn, north Wales. Firefighters managed to rescue Ms Shiers' 15-month-old son, Charlie, and his father, Liam Timbrell, 23, but they died later in hospital.

As the blaze consumed the building, Liam dialled 999 and shouted: 'Oh my God, oh my God, we're going to die.'

He also said: 'Help, help. Someone has done it on purpose. We're inside the flat.'

Rescued from the burning flat, he told a paramedic: 'It was arson, she did it, Mel did it.' It was reported that he said this two or three times.

He was very badly burned but alert and awake. He asked: 'Babies, are the babies okay?'

Then he added: 'I heard a woman shouting in the street.'

Asked by the paramedics what he meant, he replied: '"I'm going to set fire to the house" – yes, yes I heard this woman shouting she was going to set fire to the house.'

He had told a neighbour the same thing: 'I heard a woman shouting in the street: "I am going to set fire to your house." It was Mel. She said I am going to burn the house down.'

A police community support officer spoke to him and Timbrell said: 'She was shouting through the letter box: "I am going to burn your house down."'

Asked if he recognized the voice, Timbrell said: 'Yes, it was Mel from the downstairs flat.'

Threats of arson

Their downstairs neighbour, 43-year-old Melanie Smith, was a heavy-drinking, jobless mother of five. There had been an ongoing row between Smith and Lee-Anna, who Smith accused of being noisy and untidy.

On 1 September, Smith told Ms Shiers' friend, Stacey Brady, that she was going to 'make Lee-Anna's life hell'. She was ranting about her leaving cigarette butts outside the front door and shouted up at Lee-Anna: 'I am going to set your house on fire with you and your kids in it.'

Four days later, Lee-Anna's brother, Michael, called to see his sister and she told him that, when the defendant was drunk, she made threats to burn her house down, saying: 'I have threatened to burn someone else's house down and I will do the same to you.'

The manager of the Vegas Bar in Rhyl, Yvette Giblin, told police that on 13 October she heard the defendant rowing with her boyfriend, Steven Clarkson. She claims Smith said in a raised voice: 'You're shagging the woman upstairs. I will burn the house down with her and the kids in it.'

Previously, when Smith and Clarkson had been refused service in a pub, she said: 'I'm going to f***ing torch this place' and stormed out of the door in a temper.

She also believed that Clarkson was having an affair with Samantha Schofield after he had stayed at her house in August after he and Smith had had a row. Smith had vandalized Clarkson's car when it was parked outside, bending the windscreen wipers and wing mirrors, and throwing a pink milkshake at the windscreen. Some 20 matches were scattered outside, some spent, along with a matchbox.

Smith then had two conversations with Ms Schofield's sister, Amy, where she said she was 'going to set fire to Sam's house'. She also said that she had nearly set fire to the house but was 'too drunk to ignite the matches'. When it was pointed out to her that Ms Schofield had two children living with her who 'had done nothing wrong', Smith replied: 'I'm not finished with Sammy yet and I can't make any promises.'

The day before the fatal fire, Smith told her friend Pamela Handley she was going to 'torch or bomb' her landlord's flat and that he was not going to get any money from her rent.

On the morning of 19 October, Smith went to Chantelle's Hair Salon, where hairdresser Sophie Griffiths noticed she smelled of alcohol and was complaining about her flat. She said it was too small and that she did not like her neighbours or landlord, adding: 'To be honest, I wish they'd burn it to the ground because the council would have to put me up then.'

Binge drinker

That night, after having ten alcoholic drinks, Smith seems to have been incensed by a pushchair left in the shared hallway and set fire to it. The noise of the television and the couple upstairs making love also seems to have annoyed her. After starting the fire, Smith got into bed with Clarkson, so that she would appear to be a victim.

Smith claimed that she had been asleep and was awoken by thick black smoke. She and Clarkson then escaped through the bedroom window. Smith was outside in her underwear and was given a blanket to cover herself, while Clarkson got on to a flat roof at the back of the premises with other people to try to help the people above escape.

Meanwhile, two neighbours also tried to rescue the family. One of them, ex-policeman Peter Bailey, was watching TV when he heard banging noises and his wife shouted that the house over the road was on fire.

'I went outside and saw that the front door of the house was well ablaze. There were loads of people in the street with black acrid smoke pouring out of the house,' he said.

The front door was 'a ring of fire' with black smoke billowing out.

'The heat was intense with the fire raging, it was well under way,' he said.

He climbed on to the flat roof at the back with the help of a neighbour's ladder. When he put his hand against the window pane of the upstairs flat, he could feel the intense heat coming from inside.

'There was no way I could get in,' he said.

Joe Shelley was on his way to meet friends when he heard a woman's voice shouting: 'We cannot get out.'

He opened the front door of the house and was surprised at how much fire there was in the hallway. He said: 'I thought of going to try and help, but in the time I was thinking that, flames came towards the door and spiralled upwards.'

The flames made 'a massive whoosh sound' as they came out of the front door. The best he could do was to call the emergency services and run home to get a torch. When he returned, he saw a man inside the property but could not get close to the window.

In his 999 call, Shelley said that the victims were unable to break the window to escape. 'I don't think that they will be able to breathe much longer,' he said.

Smith denied causing the fire or making threats and added: 'I would never burn anyone. You have got to be pretty sick and crazy and beyond evil to do something like this.'

In court, she said that all 21 prosecution witnesses, including a firefighter and a police officer, were lying and plotting against her. Only a 'sick and evil person' would threaten to start fires in houses with children inside.

'Everyone is pointing the finger at me. On my kids' lives, I never did anything to that flat. That is from the bottom of my heart. I would not do that to my worst enemy,' she said.

Smith was sentenced to life in prison, serving a minimum of 30 years. Her ex-husband, Paul Smith, was not unhappy about the news. 'That evil woman deserves to rot in hell,' he said.

He told the *Daily Mail* that she had been cruel to her own children. She stubbed cigarettes out on her baby son's forehead, hacked off her toddler daughter's blond hair, scalded her with boiling water and locked her in an understairs cupboard as punishment, then abandoned them when they were still very young.

Her daughter, by then grown up, said: 'She was a mother from hell to me – and she still is. Spending the rest of her life in prison won't come close to what she deserves.'

CHAPTER 35

Ronald Baquiran Bae

4 January 2013

Some people turn psycho under the influence of drink and drugs. Forty-one-year-old Ronald Bae was high on alcohol and crystal meth when he walked out of the front door of his house in the village of Tabon I in the Philippines and started shooting up the neighbourhood, killing eight and wounding a further 12.

'He was a good man and father,' his wife, Elena, said, 'until he started using drugs again.'

She said she never thought her husband would end up killing people. Although they had fights and he sometimes hit her, her husband never aimed his gun at her, she added.

But she admitted that there were instances when Bae acted strangely, something that she blamed on the effects of drugs. 'He would talk to himself. Sometimes his eyes would roll upward,' she said.

Once she saw Bae talking to a wall in their house, saying things like 'I am the devil.' He also claimed he saw shadows peering at him, Elena recalled.

Mass of contradictions

Bae was the son of Rodolfo Bae, a former police chief of Imus City, Cavite Province on the southern shores of Manila Bay, though he claimed to have been adopted and wanted to find his real father. He was a former member of the village council until he ran, and failed in his bid, to be the village chief of Tabon I in 2010 under the campaign name 'bossing'. He was known as a local 'Robin Hood', though some found him to be the neighbourhood bully. He made his living buying and selling used cars and breeding fighting cocks.

The couple had a big fight. Elena said Bae's assistant, 27-year-old John Paul Lopez, came to visit them and that he and Bae had drunk heavily and used drugs.

'He was jealous of John Paul. I said: "Oh, no, dad,"' Elena said.

Then Bae started hitting her on the head. When it looked like he was about to draw his gun, Elena collected their children and barricaded them in a room until Bae and Lopez left.

'It was as if he had been possessed, as if he had become a demon,' Elena recalled.

According to witnesses, Bae's face looked blank as he shot at his victims with a .45-calibre Colt 1911 handgun. He also had licences for an M16 and an AK-47. He was assisted by Lopez, who helped reload the weapon whenever it ran out of bullets.

First, Bae shot a dog at his neighbour's house. He then shot its owner, 55-year-old Alberto Fernandez, who had looked out from his veranda after the initial shot.

'Bae then walked away casually, without any word or facial expression,' said witness Willy Salvador, a resident of the area. He said no one had dared oppose the gunman who 'fired at anything that moved'.

Wearing just a sando [a sleeveless vest] and a pair of shorts, Bae walked towards a store, looking for his neighbour, Berto Caimol. When he was told that Berto wasn't around, Bae then directed his rage at Caimol's three children. He shot and killed seven-year-old Michaella Andrea and wounded her two younger siblings – her two-year-old sister and four-year-old brother, who was one of the gunman's godsons.

Maita Lacorte, the uncle of the three children who were shot, said: 'I could not do anything. I could hear them screaming and I heard the shots.'

As Bae closed in on his house, he fled with his wife and their four children, two grandchildren and three nieces through the muddy fishpond behind their house, towards an open rice field.

'He was shooting at us as we were running,' he said.

They sought cover in the tall cogon grass

'I told the children not to make any noise. They cried quietly,' Lacorte recalled. Had he not been home, he said, 'my family would have been wiped out.'

Later he saw the bullet-riddled cushions that the other children had apparently used to protect themselves during the attack.

'It must have been the eldest who covered them with the cushions,' he said.

Acts of a madman

Based on the residents' accounts, the gunman had walked approximately 200 m (650 ft) from his home to a public market, passing at least 70 houses and shooting more people. Other victims included Boyet Toledo, 44; Irene Funelas, 38; Al Drio, 20; Rhea de Vera, 34, who was six months pregnant when she was shot in the stomach, and her daughter Jan Monica, three. The foetus also died.

Before she died, Rhea made a frantic call for help to her mother, Baby Alberto, who heard screams and gunshots.

'She said: "Please, don't! Please don't!"' Alberto heard her daughter pleading to the gunman. She said her daughter was found dead in the bathroom hugging her three-year-old daughter.

'There was no screaming. We locked all doors and windows as soon as we heard the gunfire from the other street. It turned into a ghost town,' said resident, Arvin Aquitel.

The police turned up and asked Bae to surrender. He refused and shot back. In the ensuing gunfight, Bae was shot dead.

'He just shot at anyone he saw,' said provincial governor, Jonvic Remulla. 'You could see that these were really acts of a madman. He even killed the dog.'

After the shooting, Lopez disappeared. A reward was offered, and he was turned over to the authorities by his relatives that same evening.

Lopez said that Bae had killed before. He led the police to the shallow grave and told police that the skeletal remains belonged to a certain Teodulo Villanueva, who was last seen alive with Bae in 2004. Villanueva and Bae allegedly fought over illegal drug deals.

Lopez also said he acted under duress when he helped Bae. He said that Bae did not fire his gun down to the last bullet, but 'kept one bullet and threatened to use it on me' if he did not reload the gun for him. The authorities, however, did not buy this and Lopez was charged with multiple murders for his wilful participation in the crime.

CHAPTER 36

Aaron Alexis

16 September 2013

Thirty-four-year-old lone gunman Aaron Alexis killed 12 people and injured three others in a mass shooting at the headquarters of the US Naval Systems Command (NAVSEA) inside the Washington Navy Yard in Washington DC on 16 September 2013 before being shot dead. It was the second-deadliest mass murder on a US military base after the Fort Hood massacre in November 2009.

Alexis was born in Queens in 1979. An African American, he grew up in a part of the borough that was home to South Asians, Hispanics and Orthodox Jews, and he embraced all things Thai while living in Fort Worth. He worked as a waiter at a Thai restaurant, studied the language and regularly chanted and meditated at Buddhist temples.

In 2004, according to a Seattle police report, he walked out of his grandmother's home one morning, pulled a .45-calibre pistol from his waistband and fired three rounds, two at the rear tyres of a construction worker's car and one into the air. The construction manager told the police he thought Alexis was frustrated with the parking situation outside the work site. But Alexis told the police that he had had an anger-fuelled blackout and could not remember firing the weapon until about an hour later.

He said he had been in New York during the 9/11 attacks on the World Trade Center in 2001 and told a detective 'how those events had disturbed him'. His father told investigators that Alexis had problems associated with post-traumatic stress disorder and had been an 'active participant' in rescue attempts on 11 September. He was charged with malicious mischief, but the charge was later dismissed.

Alexis did not mention this when he joined the US Navy in 2007, serving in Fleet Logistics Support Squadron 46 at Naval Air Station Joint Reserve Base Fort Worth, Texas. However, this was flagged up after a check on the FBI database. Alexis explained that he had not mentioned the incident as the charge had been dropped. According to Alexis, he had had an altercation with the construction worker 'and retaliated by deflating [his] tires'. There was no mention of him having used a firearm.

A report by the Office of Personnel Management, the federal agency responsible for conducting background checks on government employees, concluded: 'The subject committed this offence because he was retaliating for being intimidated by the male person. The subject does not intend to repeat this type of behavior because he would avoid any confrontation and notify authorities if a similar situation were to occur in the future.'

Consequently, the Navy gave him secret-level security clearance. Although Alexis's work in Fleet Logistics Support Squadron 46 did not require secret-level security clearance, new recruits are often put through the process in case they should need it in the future. Military security clearances of the kind granted to Alexis are primarily designed to detect whether a recruit is susceptible to disloyalty or bribery from an enemy force.

Holes shot in the ceiling

In the Navy, he became an aviation electrician's mate, fixing electrical systems on aeroplanes, and he attained the rank of petty officer third class. He was awarded the National Defense Service Medal and the Global War on Terrorism Service Medal, two standard military honours.

However, during his time in the service, there was 'a pattern of misbehavior'. In 2010, he was arrested in Fort Worth for discharging a firearm. At the time, he was living in an apartment complex called Orion at Oak Hill. His upstairs neighbour called the police after she heard a pop, saw dust fly and noticed holes in her floor and ceiling. She told the police that

Alexis had confronted her in the parking lot about making too much noise, and she felt threatened by him.

Alexis later told an officer that he had been cleaning his gun and it had accidentally discharged. The officer asked him why he did not call the police or check on the resident above him. He replied that he did not think the bullet went through the ceiling because he could not see any light through the hole. The officer noted that the gun had been taken apart and was covered in oil.

The father of the woman in the apartment above said the shot came through close to where his daughter had been sitting. She moved out after the episode as a lawyer advised the family not to press charges because she could not prove that he did it on purpose when he claimed he was cleaning his gun.

Nevertheless, Alexis left the Navy on 31 January 2011 with a general discharge under a scheme designed to downsize sections of the military considered to be overmanned. That seems to have been upgraded to an honourable discharge after he told his commanders that he wanted to go to college. At the time of his death, Alexis was working online on a bachelor's degree in Aeronautics from Embry-Riddle Aeronautical University.

From September 2012 to January 2013, Alexis worked in Japan, 'refreshing computer systems' on the Navy Marine Corps Intranet network for an HP Enterprise Services subcontracting company called The Experts. After returning from Japan, he expressed frustration to a former roommate that he hadn't been paid properly for the work he'd carried out. Another roommate of Alexis said that he would frequently complain about being the victim of racial discrimination. In July 2013, he resumed working for The Experts in the United States.

Returning to Fort Worth, he dated a Thai woman and began showing up regularly at Wat Busayadhammavanara, a Buddhist Temple in White Settlement, a suburb of Fort Worth. He had Thai friends, adored Thai food and said he always felt drawn to the culture. He regularly attended services, intoning Buddhist chants and staying on to meditate afterwards. On celebrations like the Thai New Year in April, he helped out, serving guests dressed in ceremonial Thai garb the temple provided.

At the temple, he met Nutpisit Suthamtewakul, who went on to open the Happy Bowl Thai restaurant in White Settlement in 2011. Alexis helped out at the restaurant in exchange for food and a room in Mr Suthamtewakul's house.

There, it was said, he played computer games 'at the night time and all day' on one of three computers he kept in his room, driving up the house's electricity bills. After he got a job fixing computers, the family asked him to contribute towards utility bills. He rarely paid and borrowed money often, complaining that his computer company was withholding pay.

In 2012, he went to stay in Thailand with Om Suthamtewakul, the sister of Nutpisit in the US. He stayed with her for a month and a half.

'Every day he has good mood, laughing,' she said, 'and one time we went to the market together because he understand Thai and he heard one Thai woman saying rude words about him – but he didn't get angry, he laughed and told the woman: "I understand what you said."'

Suthamtewakul said Alexis liked Thailand, loved Thai woman and wanted to go back. She said that she and Alexis went on outings in Bangkok and elsewhere, and that they went to massage parlours in the evening. She said she never saw him show cruelty.

'So I can't really believe how he can shoot those people,' she said. 'He looked kind of like, you know, bonkers, crazy, in a positive way, like funny, but… so I really can't believe this.'

Unusual problems

But there were problems. On 23 August 2013, he visited the emergency room of the Veterans Affairs' Medical Center in Providence, Rhode Island, complaining of insomnia. He was given sleep medication and told to follow up with a visit to a doctor.

Alexis also complained to Rhode Island police that people were communicating to him via the walls and ceilings of his hotel room and transmitting microwave vibrations into his body to keep him from falling asleep. The Newport authorities reported the incident to officers at the Navy base security office, but there was no follow-up because he didn't appear to pose a threat to himself or others at the time.

Two days later, Alexis arrived in Washington, DC and stayed in various hotels until, on 7 September, he moved into the Residence Inn in southwest Washington, where he stayed with five other civilian sub-contractors working for Hewlett-Packard Enterprise Services.

On 28 August, he visited the VA Hospital in Washington, where he said he hadn't been able to sleep due to his work schedule, and had his medication replenished. According to the VA, he seemed 'alert and oriented' during those visits and claimed that he didn't feel depressed, anxious or prone to violence. But something was going on.

On 14 September, he visited the Sharpshooters Small Arms Range in Lorton, Virginia, 24 km (15 miles) south of Washington. He tested out an AR-15 semi-automatic rifle, but did not seek to buy it, a lawyer for the store said. However, it was reported that Alexis was found with an AR-15 after the incident – the AR-15 is the standard rifle of the US military.

After purchasing ammunition and test-firing the AR-15, Alexis inquired about buying a handgun at the range. Since federal law does not allow dealers to sell handguns directly to out-of-state residents, the gun would have had to be shipped to a licensed dealer in his home state. That's why Alexis then selected a Remington 870 Express 12-gauge shotgun, as rifles and shotguns can be directly sold to out-of-state residents. He also bought two boxes of shells containing some 24 rounds, after passing a state and federal background check.

Curtain of fire

Sometime before 8.20am on 16 September, Alexis arrived at the Navy Yard in a rental car, using his security pass to enter. He entered Building 197 carrying a bag containing the disassembled shotgun, whose barrel and stock had been sawn down. He assembled the shotgun inside a bathroom on the fourth floor, then emerged with the gun and began shooting. Many of the people killed on the fourth floor were shot in the head at close range.

The first shot sounded distant and muffled according to Bertillia Lavern on the fourth floor, who assumed somebody downstairs was setting up for an event and had dropped a folding table. But when the bangs kept coming, Lavern recognized the sounds.

Before taking a civilian office job at NAVSEA, 39-year-old Lavern had been a Navy medical specialist, or corpsman, and had been on training

CCTV footage of Aaron Alexis during the attack.

operations with the Marines. She knew the sound of gunfire. She hit the ground and took cover under a desk with her supervisor, Andy Kelly, in a nearby cubicle. They stayed there silently as the shots continued.

Lavern remembered a bright flash of light.

'Glass shattered right by my head,' she said. 'It was on the edge of Andy's cubicle.'

She and Kelly ducked down again and waited for a break in the shooting.

'We realized then we had to get out of the building,' she said. 'Andy looked around the corner to check that the coast was clear.'

Lavern crawled to her desk to grab her identification badge and her purse. From there, she saw her colleague, 61-year-old Vishnu Pandit, who was the first person she greeted at the office each morning.

'He was down,' she said.

Pandit had been with the Navy for 30 years. Known to his co-workers as Kisan, he was the father of two and a grandfather. He had been shot in his left temple.

Using tissues from his desk, Lavern pressed her hand against his head, silently praying.

'I felt him breathe,' she said.

She felt for his pulse and found it surprisingly strong.

'We need help now!' she told Kelly. He ran for help while she stayed behind, tending to Pandit. She still did not know where the gunman was.

'Stay with me,' she told Pandit. 'I'm right here.'

She told him that God loved him, that his friends loved him, that they wanted him to stay with them.

'We don't want you to go,' she told him.

Three security guards arrived. They carried Pandit to an office chair, rolled him to the stairs and strapped him into an evacuation chair used to help disabled people to go downstairs in a hurry. But it was no help.

'We lifted, dragged the chair down the stairs,' she said.

At every floor, she said, she checked his pulse. It remained strong.

When they got to the second floor, she said, the security guards' radios came to life. 'The shooter was on the first floor,' it said. 'On the west side.'

That was where they had been heading.

Continuing downstairs, they escaped through a side door, where they found a security guard in an unmarked car. With Lavern and Pandit on board, they escaped from the Navy Yard, stopping at a street corner a few blocks away. With a gunman on the loose, the security guard had to get back to his post and he asked police there to get an ambulance immediately. But when Lavern eased her friend on to the pavement, his pulse was gone.

Man down

Across the street, James Birdsall was having his morning coffee in his office on the 11th floor at Parsons, an engineering company. As he and his colleagues watched the police cars screaming toward the Navy Yard, Birdsall noticed a man lying down on the street corner below at New Jersey Avenue and M Street.

He assumed someone had had a heart attack. His company had trained him to use a defibrillator, but the man was all the way across the street and there was already a woman giving CPR.

'But I thought, "If don't do this now, I'm going to look back and say I should have,"' Birdsall said, so he grabbed the office defibrillator and ran.

Birdsall knelt at Pandit's head, while Lavern pumped at his chest. He saw the gunshot wound as he attached the defibrillator pads to the man's chest. But the machine indicated that he should not administer a shock, so Lavern continued giving CPR.

Within two minutes of being dispatched, an ambulance arrived. Lavern asked to go to the hospital with him, but a detective told her she needed to give a police report instead. She removed Pandit's badge and gave it to rescue workers, so they would know who he was.

Pandit was pronounced dead on arrival at George Washington University Hospital, where Dr Babak Sarani, the hospital's director of trauma and acute care surgery, called the injury 'not survivable'.

'This injury was not survivable by any stretch,' a medical official told reporters. 'The patient was dead on the way to the hospital.'

At Pandit's funeral on 19 September, Lavern said: 'He was a good friend. He was the sweetest man.'

While Lavern escaped the Navy Yard with Pandit, Alexis continued firing on the third floor and in the lobby. At some point, Alexis shot and killed a security officer and took the officer's Beretta 9mm semi-automatic pistol, using it after running out of ammunition for his shotgun.

'I heard three gunshots, pow, pow, pow, straight in a row,' said Patricia Ward, a logistics management specialist from Woodbridge, Virginia, who was in the cafeteria on the first floor when the shooting started. 'About three seconds later, there were four more gunshots, and all of the people in the cafeteria were panicking, trying to figure out which way we were going to run out.'

A NAVSEA employee described encountering a gunman wearing all-blue clothing in a third-floor hallway, saying, 'He just turned and started firing.' At one point during the shooting, one man was hit by a 'stray bullet' in an alleyway.

At 8.23am, the first calls to 911 were made. Six minutes later, a four-person, active-shooter response team was deployed into the building. Around that time, Alexis was still firing shots on both the third and fourth floors.

'He was shooting down from above the people,' one law enforcement officer said. 'That is where he does most of his damage.'

Alexis was shot dead by the police at around 9am. He was found to have three weapons on him – an AR-15 assault rifle, a shotgun and a semi-automatic pistol.

Alexis seems to have been estranged from his family. His brother-in-law said it had been five years since Alexis had seen his sister.

'No one saw it coming, no one knew anything, so all of this is just shocking,' he said.

'To the families of the victims, I am so, so very sorry that this has happened. My heart is broken,' said Alexis's mother. 'I don't know why he did what he did, and I'll never be able to ask him why. Aaron is now in a place where he can no longer do harm to anyone, and for that I am glad.'

The shooting had taken place just a few kilometres from the White House and about 1 km (0.6 miles) from the Capitol building.

CHAPTER 37

Darren Deon Vann

2014

Nineteen-year-old Afrikka Hardy and her friend Shameeka Cunningham ran an online escort agency in Gary, Indiana. On 17 October 2014, Hardy responded to a client using the handle 'Big Boy Appetite'. She texted Cunningham to say that she was meeting the 'john' in a Motel 6 in nearby Hammond.

When Hardy did not text again to say that the encounter was over, Cunningham called her cell phone. There was no answer, so Cunningham texted her. The response she received was 'unusual' and Cunningham suspected that it had come from the male client. She and a male friend went to the room in the Motel 6 and found Hardy's naked body in the bathtub. She had been strangled. The bed had been separated from the headboard, indicating that there had been a violent struggle.

The following day, examination of the cell phone records of the man who had answered Hardy's ad led them to the West-Gary home of Darren Deon Vann, who had Hardy's phone. Vann expressed surprise that he had been caught so quickly.

Video footage from the hotel showed Vann arriving in his blue Jeep and entering Hardy's room at the time of the slaying. Vann admitted to the police that he had responded to an ad posted under the name 'Octavia', driven to the motel and killed Hardy while they were having sex. He said that 'the sex was getting rough and she started fighting with him', so he strangled her, first with his hands and then with a cord, before placing her body in the bath tub. He then turned on the shower and left.

In an effort to make a deal with the prosecutors to avoid the death penalty, he said that, so far that year, he had killed six other women and led them to the abandoned buildings where he had dumped their bodies around Gary, a once-vibrant city that had become synonymous with the rust belt.

Weird nutcase

Vann's troubles seem to have begun in 1993 when he had received an 'other than honourable' discharge from the United States Marine Corps at the age of 22. Soon after, he married a woman 30 years his senior. Her son was not happy with this.

'The guy is a nutcase. He is. And I'd watch him,' he said. 'I'd never allow him near my kids or in my home, because he just freaked me out.... He was strange, he was weird.'

Vann's own brother said much the same thing and moved to keep his two daughters away from him.

The son said things 'went downhill' for Vann after he got fired from a temp agency providing maintenance and security work, adding he had trouble finding good work after that. Eventually, the couple moved from Gary to Austin, Texas, where the son found the couple 'living in poverty'.

In April 2004, according to a police affidavit, Vann threatened to burn down or blow up the home of a man who he believed was sheltering his girlfriend. Then, in front of police, he 'grabbed her and told the police to back up or he would burn himself and [the girlfriend],' the affidavit stated.

With his left arm around the woman's neck and his right hand holding a gasoline can and lighter, Vann refused to let her go until police grabbed and arrested him. He was charged with a Class D felony and spent 90 days in jail.

In December 2007, a 25-year-old woman responded to 'a service call' from Vann and went to an apartment with him. After they got inside, Vann asked her if she was a police officer. When she told him that she was not, he attacked her, repeatedly striking, choking and raping her. He pleaded guilty to the assault and was sentenced to five years. His wife, of 16 years standing, divorced him.

Darren Deon Vann used the handle 'Big Boy Appetite'.

The killings begin

Released in 2013, Vann was put on the sex offenders register as 'low risk'. He returned to Gary, where he began his murder spree. Pleading guilty to all seven murders in a plea bargain, he was sentenced to seven concurrent terms of life imprisonment without possibility of parole.

In 2021, tapes of Vann's interviews with the police were released under a Freedom of Information Act request. In them, he claimed to have killed more in Illinois than the seven he'd admitted to in Indiana. Asked where he stayed, he said: 'I don't have to stay anywhere. I get on the train. I get on the bus. I'd be like: I know I'm losing it. I try to get far away from my family when I felt myself slipping.'

On the tapes, Vann told investigators about his urge to kill and his need to travel to find his victims: 'My rages. When stuff doesn't go right, I'm looking for an out.'

On one recording, Vann referred to his 'triggers from the past' as the reason he killed. 'She struck me,' he said. 'I don't like being hit.' But in another interview, Vann told investigators that sometimes he didn't need a reason at all. 'Casper was my friend. I didn't mean to kill her… I was already angry.'

How did he pick his victims?

'They're all random. All random,' he said. 'All it does is take the wrong person to say something and it triggers something from my past.'

He referred to his murders as 'my mistakes' and told officers his rages caused him to 'go looking for an out'. Those 'outs', Vann said, included killings in California, Texas, Wisconsin, Minnesota and Michigan, but he mentioned Chicago in particular as a place where he went a lot.

During the time Vann was in jail in Texas, the number of unsolved strangulations in Chicago had dropped dramatically.

'This is all unbelievable to me,' his ex-wife said. 'A total shocker. I never knew him to be violent, never.'

CHAPTER 38

Tamara Samsonova

1995–2015

Sixty-eight-year-old Tamara Samsonova, aka Granny Ripper, was arrested after local dogs found the limbs of her friend, 79-year-old Valentina Ulanova, in the undergrowth near her block of flats in St Petersburg. When CCTV footage was checked, Samsonova was seen going in and out of her friend's flat carrying body parts in bags and a saucepan containing her head. Her diaries then revealed that she had killed up to 11 people over 20 years.

Samsonova was Valentina Ulanov's carer and she killed her after a quarrel over an unwashed cup. She put drugs in a salad she was preparing. Once Ulanov was unconscious, Samsonova cut her up with a hacksaw while she was still alive.

'I came home and put the whole pack of phenazepamum – 50 pills – into her Olivier salad,' Samsonova told the police. 'She liked it very much. I woke up after 2am and she was lying on the floor, so I started cutting her to pieces. It was hard for me to carry her to the bathroom; she was fat and heavy. I did everything in the kitchen where she was lying.'

She wrapped body parts in curtains and put them in plastic bags before dumping them near a pond in Dimitrova Street. Her hips and legs only made it as far as the back yard. The head and hands were boiled in a large saucepan. These have not been found by the police. Nor have the internal organs. It is thought that they were thrown in the garbage skip, which was collected the following Saturday, though equally Samsonova might have eaten them.

She made seven trips outside carrying body parts. CCTV showed a figure in a blue raincoat dragging bags that left a trail of blood. When dogs sniffed out the remains, the police began a major manhunt. A social worker first reported Mrs Ulanova missing after Samsonova refused her entry to the apartment.

The dismembered torso of a man – minus his arms, legs and head – had been found in the same street 12 years earlier. The victim's business card and other evidence linking Samsonova to the murder were found in her flat.

Incriminating diaries

Among her collection of books on black magic and astrology, detectives found diaries, whose entries were in Russian, French and English. They included an account of the murder of two of her former lodgers.

'I killed my tenant, Volodya, cut him into pieces in the bathroom with a knife, put the pieces of his body in plastic bags and threw them away in different parts of Frunzensky district,' she wrote.

A 44-year-old native of Norilsk, Sergei Potynavin, was killed after an argument on 6 September 2003. She then dismembered his body and dumped the body parts in plastic bags.

Such chilling confessions were found among more mundane entries saying that she slept badly, skipped eating or taking her medicine. One read: 'I woke at 5am. I am drinking coffee. Then I do work around the house.' It went on to say that she went out to buy marshmallow. Another entry makes it clear she liked living with Mrs Ulanova, who she called Valya, even saying: 'I love Valya.'

The diaries also included poems, songs, reflections on life and descriptions of her victims' tattoos. The most gruesome entries described how she ate some of her victims.

The police also found a knife and a saw, and there were spots of blood in the bathroom. The former hotel worker admitted to 11 murders, without giving details. It was thought that she had indeed eaten some body parts from her victims, showing a particular penchant for gouging out their lungs and eating them.

It was feared that Samsonova had also disposed of her husband, who she reported missing in 2005. She told the police that he had met another woman. At the time he disappeared, neighbour Marina Krivenko recalled: 'We had some coffee in her kitchen, and we chatted. She already looked strange then. She told me about her husband, that he left home and did not come back. And at that moment I noticed some kind of pleasure in Tamara's eyes.'

Samsonova's mother-in-law also disappeared and she admitted to an old school friend, 67-year-old Anna Batalina, that she was suspected of killing her. Mrs Batalina was also thought to have been in danger after Samsonova flew into a rage with her, screaming: 'I'll kill you. I'll cut you to pieces. I will throw the pieces out for the dogs. Don't make me angry.'

Mrs Krivenko had known Samsonova for 15 years and said that she was very interested in the bloodthirsty killer, Andrei Chikatilo.

'She gathered information about him and how he committed his murders,' the neighbour said.

For years, she had boasted to friends that, 'one day I will be popular and famous'. She told them she would one day cause a 'sensation' without explaining how or why.

Mrs Krivenko reported other eccentric behaviour.

'I came to live here with my husband,' she said. 'I used to go to Tamara's flat and call from her phone. She looked a lot better 15 years ago, and her flat, too, was a lot more attractive than now. She looked after her appearance and had this weird habit of sitting topless with her back to the window, making sure that her silhouette was seen by the neighbours.'

Apparently, Mr Krivenko found this rather appealing. Mrs Krivenko also admitted lending Samsonova a hacksaw some years earlier, which she never returned.

Fame at last

Despite facing the death penalty, Samsonova was more concerned about the publicity her arrest had attracted. She told reporters: 'I knew you would come. It's such a disgrace for me, all the city will know.'

However, she bore no hostility towards newsmen, blowing a kiss to them. She refused to take the charges seriously. When the judge, Roman

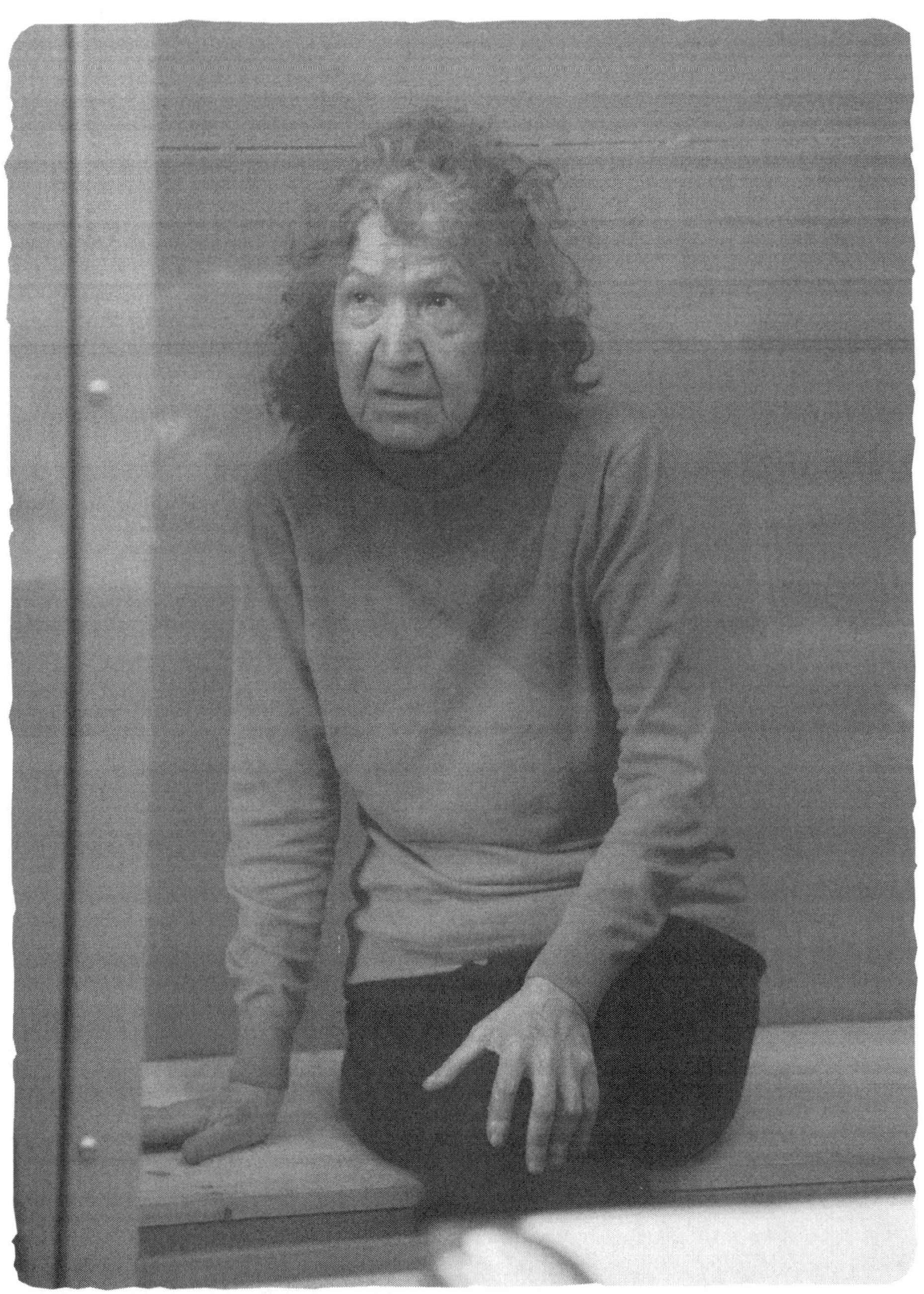

Tamara Samsonova, the carer who killed.

Chebotaryov, asked her to address the court, she said: 'It's stuffy in here, can I go out?'

She seemed to be relieved to have been caught, telling the judge: 'I was getting ready for this court action for dozens of years. It was all done deliberately… This is no way to live. With this last murder, I closed the chapter.'

The judge said: 'I am asked to detain you. What do you think?'

'You decide, your honour,' she replied. 'After all, I am guilty and I deserve punishment.'

When told that she would remain in custody, she beamed and clapped her hands.

While admitting to murdering Mrs Ulanova and others, Samsonova refused to co-operate with police over other suspected killings. Although the police did not rule out further charges, without finding the body parts prosecution would be problematic.

'We may never know the extent of this granny's killings,' one source close to the investigation said.

After the hearing, Samsonova was taken under guard on a high-security train nearly 1,600 km (1,000 miles) to a psychiatric prison hospital in Kazan, capital of Tatarstan, for assessment. This was where Joseph Stalin's secret police used to lock up political prisoners. It then became the Kazan Psychiatric Hospital of Special Purpose with Intensive Guarding.

CHAPTER 39

Shawn Grate

2006–2016

At 6.47am on 13 September 2016, a young woman called 911 in Ashland, Ohio. After a long silence, the despatcher heard a woman's voice whisper: 'I've been abducted.'

In a voice so quiet it was barely audible, a woman said she was lying in bed next to her kidnapper. When he had fallen asleep, she had wriggled free and swiped his cell phone off the nightstand.

'He's got a Taser,' she said. 'Please hurry!'

She said that she was being held in one of two yellow houses across the street from a laundromat, just a few blocks from downtown Ashland, a small midwest city that had seen better days.

'Who abducted you?' the despatcher asked. Straining to hear the reply, the operator made out the name, Shawn Grate.

Three officers were sent. Circling the buildings and peering through the windows, they could see no sign of anyone. As they headed back to their black and whites, one of the cops retried a rear door. Suddenly, he saw a woman's hand pressed flat against a windowpane. Free now, she had accidentally Tasered her captor.

The woman was naked and there was extensive bruising on her legs. A restraint hung from her arm.

Inside, the police found a nightmare scenario. Dirty clothes and trash filled the rooms, in places piled to the ceiling. She had been held there and sexually assaulted for three days.

'The best way to describe her is complete and utter shock,' said Detective Curt Dorsey. 'She was just frozen… a face I'll never forget.'

Terrible ordeal

As she was the victim of a sex attack, the 38-year-old woman was not named and appeared as 'Jane Doe' in court. She said she had first met 40-year-old Grate that summer at the Ashland Salvation Army Ray & Joan Kroc Corps Community Center. There, they would share lunch and go on long walks together, frequently discussing the Bible and occasionally playing tennis. Despite Grate's attempts to sexually engage with her, her relationship with him was described as completely platonic. She said she did not believe in pre-marital sex and refused even to exchange phone numbers or let him into her apartment.

On 11 September, he persuaded her to walk back to his house to pick up some clothes from his mother and sister to give to her. She was in his room reading the Bible when he pulled it out of her hands. When she looked up at him, he said: 'You're not going anywhere.'

'I tried to push him away,' she said. 'I tried to kick, punch, but everything I did, he just did it so much harder back.'

Doe said she continued to fight until Grate started choking her.

'I knew I couldn't get out of it,' she said.

Asked how he sexually assaulted her on the first night, she said: 'In every way imaginable.'

She said Grate tied her up at least three times 'in weird positions or to the bed'. At one point, she said he put a restraint around her neck and told her she would strangle herself if she tried to move. Doe said Grate continually assaulted and raped her while she was awake. He also shaved a heart in her pubic hair. After the forensic examiner had finished with her, she was allowed to take a shower and given a razor to shave it off.

Grate told a different story. They had been discussing marriage.

'I did one little thing,' he said. 'We have a good relationship... had. I guess it's all up to her now.'

He said that they had sex.

'I thought it was mutual,' he said in the interview. 'She started flipping out.'

He admitted that he had 'lost control' and that the situation 'got out of hand'.

This was somewhat disingenuous as Grate was already a serial killer.

Hidden closet

During his interrogation, Detective Kim Mager asked him about the disappearance of two other women – Elizabeth Griffith and Stacey Stanley Hicks. He immediately reacted to Elizabeth's name and, after a couple of hours, he admitted kidnapping her. Where was she? In a closet in an upstairs bedroom, he said. But there was no closet in the upstairs bedroom said an agent from the Ohio Bureau of Criminal Investigation, who had joined the investigation.

Returning to the house, the police found a sofa bed with articles of clothing tied to the metal frame, possibly serving as makeshift restraints. The air was putrid. Against a wall, officers observed an odd-looking wooden pole with condoms attached to its tip. It was slender and long, measuring several feet in length.

Several of these strange apparatuses were later found in other rooms in the house. More would turn up in the trailers and campsites he had occupied around the area. Grate later said he'd been using them on himself.

A strange array of clothing hung from nails and stretched from floor to ceiling in a corner of the room. Beneath the bizarre mosaic was a pile of dozens of stuffed animals.

Behind it, they discovered a can of air freshener, fly pupae on the floorboards and a dark, wooden door sealed shut with thick, black tape. Even the keyhole was covered.

When the door was opened, the foetid smell that poured out was overwhelming. They had found Elizabeth's body. The top of her head was pressed against the back wall of the closet, strands of her blond hair still visible.

Her legs were bent slightly upward, and her hands were behind her back as if they had been tied. Stacey's body was found in the basement. Both women had been strangled.

String of murders

In 2018 Grate pleaded guilty to the two murders and was sentenced to death. The following year, he pleaded guilty to the aggravated murder of Rebekah Leicy and Candice Cunningham in 2015 and the gross abuse of their corpses. They had both been strangled. Cunningham had been Grate's girlfriend for a time and her body was found behind a house they had once shared, which he had then set fire to. He was sentenced to life without parole, plus 17 years to life on three related charges, the sentences to run consecutively.

Six months later, he got another sentence of life imprisonment without parole for the murder of Dana Nicole Lowrey, a 23-year-old mother of two, in 2006. Her remains were found in neighbouring Marion County and had been unidentified since their discovery in March 2007.

Shawn Grate is escorted into the courthouse.

Grate was given a death sentence but continued to appeal against his execution.

His estranged mother said: 'He's good-looking, but the Devil's good-looking, too. He ain't [got] no red horns and all that stuff. You find out he's charming and of course that charm can charm the pants off anybody, not to be nasty, but you just know how it works.'

CHAPTER 40

Juan Carlos Hernández and Patricia Martínez

2012-2018

The couple were active in the Ecatepec de Morelos suburb of Mexico City and became known at the Monsters of Ecatepec. Juan Carlos had been brought up by a single mother who often dressed him as a girl and forced him to watch her having sex with men she brought to the house.

He also said that he was sexually abused as a child by a woman who babysat him and, at the age of ten, he fell down the stairs and suffered a traumatic brain injury.

'I was a slow learner, but after I fell off the stairs I was getting straight As,' he said. 'I don't know if my f***ing brain got inflamed, but after that moment... perfection in school. I realized things that many children don't realize at that age.'

Patricia was thought to be intellectually impaired and worked as a waitress and sometime prostitute. They met in 2008 at the bar where she worked. He was a regular customer.

He took her out and claimed to be a professional hitman, working for a 'Mr Charley from Tepito'. They lived together and moved to Ecatepec. In 2012, Juan Carlos posted a small ad in the local paper asking for domestic help, though Patricia admitted that this was designed to bring women to the house that he could rape.

A 22-year-old woman turned up. Juan Carlos explained that his wife needed someone to help with the chores as she was pregnant with their third child. She took the job.

Juan Carlos then accompanied her to the bathroom to collect some dirty clothes. He grabbed her and told her that, if she did what she was told, no harm would come to her. He then stuck his head out of the door and told Patricia to go out on the street with their youngest child.

When she returned half-an-hour later, the young woman was lying on the bathroom floor with her throat slit.

'I freaked out and told him that I was going to report him, but he told me not to be stupid, that they were going to lock us both up, and I believed him,' Patricia claimed.

He then began dismembering the body.

'Juan Carlos cut off a piece of meat from her right leg, slicing it, taking out four steaks,' said Patricia, 'and I made roast beef and my husband, Juan Carlos, and I ate from there, putting the rest of her body in a cardboard container and at night we went to throw it away in a vacant lot on Lázaro Cárdenas Street, on the tracks, in a cart. Since people knew we were garbage collectors, they didn't find it strange that we threw garbage out at night.'

Victim filleted

The second victim was a neighbour's daughter who frequently came to the couple's home to inhale solvents. The girl was practically a child and had been invited by Patricia. Juan Carlos 'approached her and began to tell her that she was very pretty,' Patricia said. He tied her up and laid her down on the mattress. Then, he asked Patricia to 'kiss her and touch her sexually'. She refused and left with her son.

When they returned, she found the girl with her throat slit and 'cut in half'. Patricia protested because the bathroom was full of blood. Juan Carlos said: 'What do you want? The bathroom is small.'

They covered the body with cardboard because the victim's father came to visit them. When he left 'very drunk', Juan Carlos 'filleted' the girl and 'took a kilo of steak from her'.

'I made roast beef that we accompanied with a sauce that I bought at Doña Lupita's store,' said Patricia. 'I also bought sacks of sugar or flour, and when I returned, the arms were already cut in two parts, he also removed the legs… he also removed the head, leaving only the torso and the tailbone.'

They put the remains in the sacks and went to throw them away in the vacant lot in Lázaro Cárdenas.

The couple moved to another house, but since the owner was always around, 'nothing could be done'. They tried two more neighbourhoods. In the first, the owner of the house 'was more attentive' and, in the second, there were security cameras. However, it was there that they met three of their future victims.

Thorax in a pot

In December 2015, they moved to a house on Monte Blanco Street. 'The opportunities we had to kill were when the landlady went to see her sister who was sick,' said Patricia. That month, one of the women they had met up with in the previous neighbourhood visited their home to sell them a blender. They invited her in and gave her Rancho Viejo tequila.

'When she was already very drunk,' they laid her down on the bed. The two of them touched her and kissed her. The woman refused their advances. But Juan Carlos raped her, then took her to the bathroom. Patricia left with the children, 'so they wouldn't see what we were doing'.

She returned 30 minutes later to find Juan Carlos listening to music on headphones, while he cut up the body with chicken shears.

'He put the thorax and a piece of fat in a pot,' Patricia said. 'I fried that in oil. Its meat was very good because it had a lot of wine, and we ate it… He put the bones in a pink grocery bag, to throw them in the vacant lot.'

That afternoon, Patricia invited a neighbour to come to the house for a drink. Juan Carlos was watching television in the bedroom when the neighbour arrived, accompanied by her ten-year-old daughter.

When Juan Carlos heard that there were visitors, he came through, sat next to the neighbour and began caressing her legs, 'asking her if it didn't bother her'. The neighbour said no. Juan Carlos then ordered Patricia to caress her too.

'I asked her if she wanted to experiment, and she said yes, that if in this life you don't experiment, you're not living,' Patricia said.

They had sex 'for about 30 minutes'. When everything was over, the neighbour looked upset. She was about to leave, but Juan Carlos told her: 'You can see that you are not going to leave because you are going to report me.'

They began to struggle. He threw her down on the bed and asked Patricia to tie her feet. Then he carried her to the bathroom and slit her throat.

The next day, Patricia went to the market to buy food. When she returned, she found the girl, the victim's daughter, crying 'because Juan Carlos had already sexually abused her'.

'I didn't see how he killed her, because I was making the food,' Patricia said. 'We ate her roasted meat.'

Feeding frenzy

In November 2017, they moved to Playa Tijuana, where they claimed their next victim, the 16-year-old daughter of the woman who had tried to sell them the blender, who they had killed earlier. The girl came to see them frequently because 'at home we gave her food and for her vice'.

One night, the girl stayed overnight and had sex with Juan Carlos. She woke up still drugged and resumed inhaling solvents. Juan Carlos was upset that the girl was still in the house, so he cut her throat, 'let her bleed and cut her into pieces… fat, meat'.

The meat, Patricia said, 'he gave it to the dogs on the street' and kept 'the bones to sell'. Apparently, he gave them to a *santero* – that is an artist who creates religious images – that he had met at a Mexibús station. The rest were placed in plastic buckets, which they covered with cement. These were taken to a new home on Isla Street that they were about to move into when they were arrested.

In her statement, Patricia detailed four more murders of women Juan Carlos had raped and dismembered, keeping the remains of one of them in the fridge.

'When she tried to escape, we grabbed her and I helped her tie her feet with a strap that Juan Carlos had in the fridge and with a rope,' Patricia said.

In all, they killed between ten and 20 women. They were caught when stopped pushing a baby buggy containing human body parts.

CHAPTER 41

Óscar Garciá Guzmán

2006–2019

The Monster of Toluca (the capital of México state in central Mexico), Guzmán began work at the age of 16 by killing his own father. This was only discovered after he had been arrested in 2019 and confessed patricide on the phone to his mother. Then, he formally admitted his guilt to the authorities.

Six years after his dad's death, in 2014 when he was 24, Guzmán became infatuated with a girl named Mónica at a high school in the suburb of Otzolotepec and began stalking her. He broke into her home and was rifling through her belongings when he was caught by her father, who he stabbed and finished off with an axe.

When Mónica returned home, he abducted her, taking her to his home in Villa Santin, where he held her, repeatedly sexually assaulted her and tortured her for two days, before beating her to death two days before her birthday. Then he cut up her body, putting the pieces in cardboard boxes, which he threw into a ravine.

Five years later, 27-year-old psychology student Adriana González Hernández introduced Guzmán to her family as her 'boyfriend'. A few days later, she went missing. Guzmán later confessed to holding her alive for nearly a year.

Then on 9 February 2019, 25-year-old criminology and law student, Marth Patricia 'Patty' Nava Sotelo, disappeared in nearby Huixquilucan. For months, she been complaining that she was being stalked by someone in a black truck. Drugged, she was held for several days before she died.

Guzmán was at the Technological University of Mexico with 23-year-old psychology student Jéssica Guadalupe Orihuela, who had complained that he was harassing her before she disappeared on 24 October 2019. Her family figured that he was responsible and went to his house to confront him on several occasions. He denied seeing her and threatened them if they did not stop bothering him.

Claiming that they had seen her through the window, they went to the police who said there was nothing they could do until they got a court order. This took four days. By that time, Guzmán had fled. Searching his house on 30 October, the police found Jéssica's body in the bathroom. She had been strangled just a few hours earlier. The bodies of the other missing women were found buried in his backyard.

On the run, Guzmán taunted the police on social media over their inability to catch him, saying he would kill again unless the safety of the cats and dog he had left behind in his house was guaranteed. But his use of the internet proved to be his downfall. He was caught after logging on to wifi at a concert in Mexico City. In all, he was sentenced to 217 years and six months in jail.

CHAPTER 42

Andrey Yezhov

2010–2020

A lifelong peeping tom, Andrey Yezhov used to spy on naked women in the bath house in his village of Sloboda in the Smolensk Oblast in western Russia on the border of Belarus. His first sexual encounter was with a dead cow. This prompted him to abuse other livestock on his family's farm.

Working on a state farm, he fell in love with a co-worker. They moved to the Kashirsky District outside Moscow, where they married. However, at the wedding reception he met a girlfriend of his brother's wife, who he started dating. She was well off and Yezhov left his wife in the dormitory where they were living and moved in with his mistress. But he did not give up his old habits of spying on women in the bath house or peeping though the windows of apartments. His wife did not know about this, but their relationship deteriorated and Yezhov spent more time in his garage drinking.

One night, he was out for a walk when he saw a light on in the window of a house and peeped in.

'On the bed, I saw an elderly woman in a nightgown. Her breasts were partially exposed. I stayed near the window for about ten minutes and did not see anyone else at home,' he said.

The 79-year-old woman was asleep. He broke in and strangled her, so that she would not scream when he raped her corpse, he said. Then, he stole her TV set.

A taste for murder

Afraid of being arrested, he waited three years before he struck again. Once again, he was out for a night-time walk and drunk on vodka when he spotted a light on in an apartment. This time, the victim was a 95-year-old woman. After he killed her, he could not get an erection, so he sodomized her repeatedly with anything to hand. Then, he stole six of her husband's medals and left. Soon after, he began planning his next attack.

On the way home from work, he saw the shutters of a window slightly open. Inside, a 60-year-old woman was lying on a couch. He broke in, strangled and raped her.

'I started to like it,' he said. 'It turned out that I was committing crimes and not being punished for it. I did not worry and did not repent that I killed grandmothers.'

Nevertheless, he took two years off. Then in 2015, while he was fixing his car, occasionally swigging from a bottle, a woman who was also drunk came into his garage and asked for a ride home. Although around 35 or 40, and too young for his taste, he decided to kill her and rape her dead body.

He offered her a drink. When she refused, he started to strangle her. She screamed, but there was no one around and he killed her. Bundling her dead body into the back of the car, he raped her. Then he stabbed her twice, drove out into the countryside and dumped her body by the roadside.

For the next four years, he took another break. Then, in 2019, he murdered and raped two women who lived on the same street – one 70, the other 75. By then, it was clear that there was a serial killer on the loose.

In January 2020, he climbed through the bedroom window of a ten-year-old girl, raped and attempted to murder her, but she was rescued by her parents. The following month, he tried to strangle a 14-year-old girl, but she fought him off.

In June, he strangled and raped an 88-year-old woman. He tried to steal her TV but found it was too heavy, so he stolen her pension book and other documents instead. After her body was found, local CCTV footage was checked. A man was seen trying to dispose of some documents in a pile of grass. When the police retrieved them, it was clear that they related to the old woman.

DNA was taken from the men in the area and Yezhov's matched samples found at three of the murder sites and from the rape of the ten-year-old. He was arrested and admitted everything but hanged himself in his cell before he could be tried.

CHAPTER 43

Shavkat Shayakhmedov

1994–2021

Known as the Zalegoshchensky Maniac or the Zalegoshchensky Beast, Shavkat Shayakhmedov was born in Uygur, a former Soviet Uzbek Republic, now part of Uzbekistan, in 1960. He claimed to have been sexually abused by a relative as a child, as serial killers often do.

After doing his national service in the Red Army, he said he was forced to leave Uygur by the locals when he refused to learn Uzbek. He moved to Istiqlol, a city in the Tajik Soviet Socialist Republic, now Tajikistan. There, he married a local woman who gave birth to twins – a son named Roman and a daughter named Ruzilya.

In the mid-1990s, the family moved on to Russia, settling in the village of Kazar in the Zalegoshchensky District of the Oryol Oblast, some 320 km (200 miles) south of Moscow, where he worked as a mechanic. A hard worker, he saved enough money to buy an apartment.

However, Shayakhmedov was a drinker and smoked marijuana. His children followed suit and there were rumours that he was sexually abusing his underage daughter – even in front of his wife, who covered up for him, it was said. Ruzilya's parents would not let her go to college and the twins were often locked in the house. Ruzilya tried to commit suicide on several occasions.

At the age of 25, Roman drank himself to death. Three months later, Ruzilya died of cirrhosis of the liver. Shayakhmedov then quit his highly paid job as a mechanic and became a plumber in a local school. The pupils called him Uncle Sasha after he gave them sweets and cigarettes. Then, he was accused of molesting a girl from a special-needs class.

A schoolgirl named Marina said: 'One day he took my friend behind a wooden toilet in the school grounds and started touching her intimate parts. She resisted, and he backed off. She told her classmates about it. But we didn't attach much importance to it.'

Brutal slayings

In April 2000, he lured a six-year-old boy into some bushes and raped him. Then, he killed the boy and threw his body down a ravine. Three years later, he came across a 32-year-old woman, who was asleep and probably drunk.

'I'm going fishing, I see a woman lying there,' he said. 'Well, men are all bastards. I wanted a freebie. Well, what can I do, undress her, that's it.'

Apparently, she did not object too vehemently, saying only 'enough' after he had finished the attack. Nevertheless, he feared she would remember his face and strangled her.

Then, he started abusing an 11-year-old boy, who lived next door and threatened to tell his grandmother. He, too, was strangled and his body buried in a forest.

In 2021, Shayakhmedov was sexually abusing another neighbour, this time a nine-year-old girl named Viktoria Gnedova. He promised to buy her a motorbike but failed to deliver.

'She got tired of my harassment,' he said. 'She says – I'll tell my mother, I'll tell my father. There was a hammer lying around, so I hit her three or four times, maybe more.'

He buried the body in the basement. But news that the girl had gone missing prompted the governor of the region to invite the public to take part in a massive search. Two sisters then came forward to say that they had been sexually assaulted by Shayakhmedov back in 2005. He was arrested and, under interrogation, admitted Viktoria's murder and showed detectives where he had hidden the body.

After he was charged, he admitted to other murders and also that he had raped three further underage girls, though his lawyer insisted that the confessions had been beaten out of him. He was sentenced to life imprisonment.

Beginning his sentence in a penal colony, he then admitted a fifth murder back in Istiqlol in 1994. He said that he had lured eight-year-old Katya Dmitrieva into his garage, where he raped and strangled her. Then he buried her body under his mother-in-law's house.

Having suffered a stroke during his initial interrogation, Shayakhmedov died of complications in 2023. His family refused to claim his body and he was buried in the penal colony.

CHAPTER 44

Roberto José Carmona

1986–2022

In Argentina, Roberto José Carmona is known as The Human Hyena and is the second longest-serving prisoner in the country's history. He became famous early in his career when his ghosted autobiography, *Yo, Carmona* (*I, Carmona*), was published in 2014.

He was born in Buenos Aires Province in 1963 to a single mother who abandoned him. At the children's home, he was beaten and starved. He suffered more abuse in a convent and, when still a child, travelled alone over 960 km (600 miles) – by bus, hitchhiking and on foot – to find his mother. Although she took him in, she was neglectful and he turned to drugs. At the age of ten, he broke into a police car and stole a .45-calibre pistol.

From then on, he was in and out of juvenile institutions and, later, prisons. In 1982, at the age of 19, he was given a ten-year sentence for aggravated robbery, kidnapping and possession of drugs.

On 10 January 1986, he was released on parole. Five days later, in the early hours of 15 January, he stopped his car to help three young people, whose car had a flat tyre. They had been out dancing. Once he had finished changing the tyre, he pulled a gun and robbed them of all their possessions. Then, he forced one of them, 16-year-old Gabriela Ceppi, into his car.

'Don't worry, I'm not a rapist,' he said.

However, after driving a few kilometres, it seems he stopped and raped her. Although he initially confessed to this, he later denied it and he was not indicted for it. He then drove on to Toledo, where apparently he sexually assaulted her again.

Following the attack, they got out of the car and crossed a fence into a field. Carmona said that Gabriela was crying and asked him what he was going to do with her. He made her kneel down and shot her in the head.

Afterwards, he picked up two hitchhikers who he forced to accompany him in an armed robbery. He was arrested after kidnapping a taxi driver and his family in order to rob them. He was put on trial. Convicted, he was given a life sentence for murder and on multiple counts of aggravated robbery and aggravated kidnapping.

Murder machine

In prison in Córdoba, he stabbed a fellow inmate because he would not 'lend him his wife for sex' when she arrived on a marital visit. The man survived, but that night while he was sleeping, Carmona threw boiling syrup in his face, disfiguring him.

Then, he stabbed to death a popular fellow prisoner. Other prisoners tried to lynch him. He was sentenced to another 16 years in prison and transferred to a prison in another province. Due to his violent nature, he ended up in a maximum-security prison, where he stabbed to death another prisoner with the sharpened end of a broomstick. He was given a second life sentence without the possibility of parole.

When refused permission to have a cell phone to stay in touch with relatives, he sewed his mouth shut. In 2011, he was officially designated a psychopath. Nevertheless, in 2014, he was given time off to visit his partner, whose mobility was limited by osteoarthritis and by having a quadriplegic son. He was allowed to go to her house for three days every four months, accompanied by prison officers.

Consequently, he was visiting his partner on 13 December 2022 when Argentina were playing Croatia in the semi-finals of the World Cup. The six prison officers accompanying him were engrossed in the match when Carmona said he was going to the lavatory and seized the opportunity to escape.

Outside the house, he stopped a taxi and stabbed the driver several times. Shoving the driver into the passenger seat, he took the wheel and drove off. But 15 minutes later, the injured driver revived and tried to seize back control of the car. In the struggle, they had a crash, which killed the cab driver. Carmona escaped unscathed.

In a supermarket, he attacked a couple with a knife and stole their car, which he later abandoned. He then approached a young woman and her mother coming out of a clinic and tried to take their car. The young woman tried to stop him and suffered cuts to her hands. They screamed; he fled.

After a massive manhunt, Carmona was captured and received a third life sentence for the murder of the cab driver. The prison guards who let him give them the slip also faced disciplinary charges.

CHAPTER 45

Ramon Escobar

2018–2023

Ramon Escobar entered the US illegally and was deported six times before he was released, pending a political asylum hearing in 2017. Along the way, he picked up six felony convictions on charges ranging from burglary to assault and criminal trespassing. He then spent a period of time in mental hospital before going on a murder spree. Even when he was caught and sentenced, he could not stop killing and went on to kill his cellmate.

'He is a violent predator,' said Captain Billy Hayes, head of the Los Angeles Police Department Robbery-Homicide Division.

Escobar's victims were largely homeless men whom he beat to death with a baseball bat or bolt-cutters.

'Nobody in their right mind would do something as vicious as this,' said Hayes.

Mentally unstable

Born into poverty in El Salvador in 1971, Escobar first entered the US illegally in the 1980s. In 1988, he was arrested and deported, but soon returned. Then, in 1995, he was convicted of burglary and sentenced to five years in prison, though he was deported again two years later.

Again, re-entering the US illegally, he was arrested for a minor offence, as well as illegal entry and sentenced to 23 months' imprisonment. While in jail, Escobar was diagnosed as a schizophrenic and transferred to the Harris County Psychiatric Center, where he remained for several months.

While making another attempt at illegal re-entry in 2012, he was caught by border security in Brownsville and detained in the county jail, where he exhibited signs of mental instability and was transferred to a prison medical facility in Springfield, Missouri. Returned to Brownsville in October 2013, he was sentenced to two years in federal prison.

Escobar entered the US illegally again in 2016 but was granted leave to appeal his deportation order and freed. He went to stay with his uncle Rogelio Escobar and his aunt, Rogelio's sister Dina, in Houston, Texas.

Psychotic behaviour

On 26 August 2018, Escobar beat his uncle to death with a police baton and disposed of his body in a dumpster. However, he left Rogelio's backpack, shoes and shirt on the porch of his home.

Two days later, Dina went to look for her brother. Escobar hid in the back of her Chevy Uplander minivan and, when she stopped, he strangled her. Leaving her body in another dumpster, he drove to Galveston, where he set fire to the vehicle. His uncle and aunt's remains were later found in landfill.

Designated a person of interest in the case, Escobar fled Texas and arrived in Los Angeles on 5 September. Three days later, he attacked a homeless man, who was sleeping under the Santa Monica pier. Despite being repeatedly struck over the head with a baseball bat and sustaining severe injuries, the victim survived. Two days later, Escobar attacked another homeless man. This time the victim died.

The following weekend, three men were attacked with a baseball bat. The perpetrator was seen rummaging through their pockets and took some of their belongings. Two of the men died.

On 20 September, a man sleeping under Santa Monica Pier was beaten to death. He was not homeless but had gone there to fish and decided to spend the night. Four days later, another man was attacked in the street in Santa Monica. This time, there were witnesses and Escobar was arrested nearby.

Interviewed by the police, Escobar said he killed some of the victims because they 'irritated him, they were disrespectful to law enforcement, or he robbed them because he needed money'.

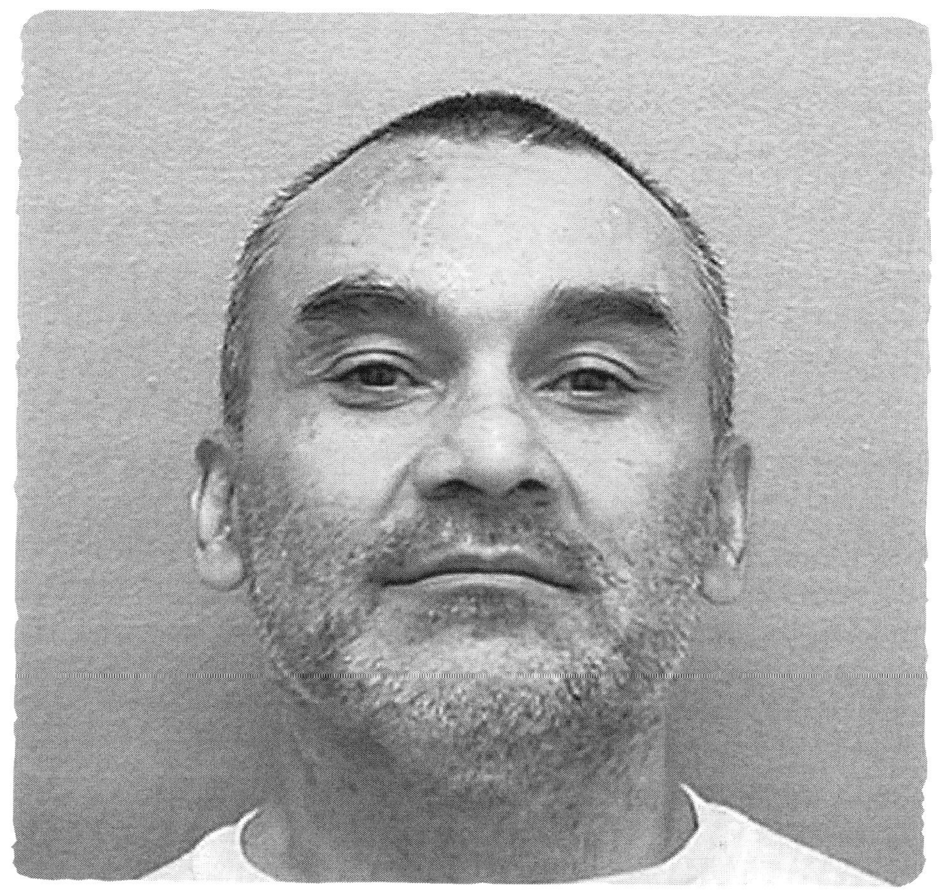

Ramon Escobar 'killed ... without a second thought'.

Escobar pleaded guilty to five murders along with seven charges of attempted murder. Via Zoom, from the courtroom in California, he pleaded guilty to the murder of his uncle and aunt, receiving two other life sentences without parole to be served consecutively in jail in California.

'This man was a monster who killed strangers and members of his own family without a second thought,' said District Attorney, Kim Ogg. 'He choked unsuspecting people to death and bludgeoned others with heavy objects, sometimes while they slept. His callous actions showed that he never cared about anyone else.'

In 2023, Escobar's cellmate, who was serving life for the aggravated sexual assault of a child, was found dead. According to court documents, Escobar admitted the homicide and wrote a note explaining why he'd done it, saying: '1) Didn't want to shower or bird bath right. 2) Didn't wanna clean cell. 3) Stank like pure s—. 4) Didn't wanna move I asked 2 or 3 times. 5) Didn't wanna take me serious so please meet the devil ha, ha.'

Index

Picture credits

Alamy: 57, 107, 116, 125, 131, 136, 153, 156, 161, 164, 171, 227

Getty Images: 39, 47, 91, 101, 104, 114, 144, 175, 191, 217

Public Domain: 52

Wikimedia Commons: 22, 75, 180, 185, 210, 222, 247